The Relevance of Kabir

Interpreting Anew the Radical 15th Century Philosopher-Poet

By Todd Vickers

---

1. http://www.therelevanceofkabir.com

Acknowledgments

While writing an online newsletter, I referenced the 15th century poet Kabir to make my own points clearer. The response from my readers gave birth to the idea to create this book. My thanks go out to those individuals who helped make this work possible, especially my dear friend, Chandra Kotaru, for his support and criticism, without which this project would not have happened. I would like to thank Gregg Elbert, who always offered considerable material support and challenging points-of-view and hosted me in his home on several occasions, creating a welcome space to complete the work. Thanks go to my uniquely beloved Sharon Schlotthauer for her love and proofreading, which made the book far better than it might have otherwise been.

Edited by: Emily Heinlen Davis
emily.heinlen@gmail.com

The translation sources for the poems used within this book are identified as follows:

Vinay Dharwadker, *The Weavers Songs* (Cyber City: Penguin Books, 2003) = TWS

Robert Bly, *The Kabir Book* (Boston: A Seventies Press Book, 1977) = TKB

Rabindranath Tagore, *Songs of Kabir* (Newburyport: Red Wheel/ Weiser, 2002) = SoK

Linda Hess and Shukdeo Singh, *The Bijak of Kabir* (Oxford: Oxford University Press, 2002) = TBoK

Foreword

Anyone who points out fault with common ideas must face opposition and even danger from the crowd. Long ago in Hindustan, a man named Kabir criticized the customs and habits that hobbled the people around him. He was bold, poor and brilliant. His lyrics are not just an invitation to self-inquiry, but a provocation to daring and open-minded people to see the elusive, yet plain facts in front of their faces. This book shines one source of light onto a unique 15th century man.

There may be as many variations of Kabir's story as there are people to tell it. He was born somewhere around 1398[i] in the last years of the Lodi Dynasty and possibly witnessed the Mughal Empire rise to power before he died. Uneducated and of low birth, he made his living by weaving. The name Kabir is one of the 100 Muslim names for God. One story suggests that he was of illegitimate birth, abandoned as a baby and had his name written on his hand. He grew to become an apostate to Islam, a choice notable for being punishable by death.[ii] He became a disciple of the Hindu Ramananda and Kabir held his Guru in esteem even after he abandoned and criticized Hinduism. If he feared the consequences of his bold words, then he did not allow that emotion to govern him. By revealing ignorance in disguise, Kabir's prose unrepentantly stripped the credibility from religious texts and those individuals possessing both spiritual authority and reputation.

As long as humans can create or be lead into error and falsehoods, we will need people like Kabir to expose the flaws. The members of any group use the desire for admiration along with the fear of disgrace to police other participants. These two separate aspects of our vanity are extremely effective as a coercive force. If vanity fails to control people, physical force and violence become another option. Groups today still deal out prestige or scorn to keep people deferential to the groups' beliefs; regardless of whether these beliefs are based on truths.

At times throughout his work, Kabir reveals the price he paid, like being insulted and beaten, to speak truthfully, particularly among the high caste. Perhaps this poet had nothing to lose since he was an untouchable, faithless bastard. As such, he could dare to say the truth. Maybe he had so much love that he felt compelled to remedy the useless human misery that he witnessed around him. Regardless of why he said what he did, those individuals who try to homogenize his verses with traditional attitudes destroy the message that he intended to convey. Our modern foolishness shows that Kabir's insights are still relevant.

Slander! Slander!
People deride me -
folks truly love
to smear and tarnish.
Slander's my father,
slander's my mother.
If your name has been blackened,
you'll go to Vaikuntha - true Name's meaning
will set itself in your mind.
There is so much calumny,
my heart's purified -
my vilifier
scrubs my clothes clean.
Whoever maligns me
is my friend -
my heart goes out
to every detractor.
The one who stops decrying me
is my real critic -
such a denouncer
vexes my life.

**Defamation's
my dearly beloved -
revilement puts me
in its debt.
Everybody
slings mud at Kabir -
my denigrator drowns,
I land on the other shore.**

TWS PP105

Kabir did not withhold when faulting someone. Even the law-abiding and charitable commonplace people did not escape Kabir's censure. His critical eye gazed on those around him without placing himself beyond reproach. The tale of *The Emperor's New Clothes* comes to mind. In it, a child speaks the truth and exposes the naïveté of a naked monarch and the deferential masses. Kabir speaks like this child. The difference being that Kabir was a man, not a fictional character, and the illusions he dispelled were not about clothing, but involved cherished beliefs. This truth provoked people to react.

We can hide as part of a crowd and abandon personal responsibility. Ideas that people hold in common have long been a powerful way of physically grouping people and religion is a case in point. Groups tend to impose norms and, as such, we assume that their ideas are good, which, in turn, suggests that the people who believe them must be good people. For members, the reward and prestige of belonging is ego fulfilling. Individuals sometimes participate in terrible things as part of a group and history affords us many examples. Most people who really think that they are good tend to dislike scrutiny that suggests there is more to them than the identity they claim.

Groups that offer rewards and punishments to their members employ the methods of animal trainers. For an animal, accomplishing the trainer's desire becomes the easiest thing it can do as it is the path of least resistance. Repetition makes the beast's responses habitual and changes its motivation from avoiding pain to seeking pleasure. Comparing people to domesticated creatures is not flattering; however, one must ask whether the suggestion is supported by observation. Let us not dismiss the animal metaphor without asking if our own bristling against it demonstrates the point.

"A horse which has been often driven along a certain road

resists the attempt to drive him in a different direction."[iii]

Bertrand Russell

If the above horse metaphor is true, then it throws into question what we call freedom and also the pursuit or satisfaction of desire. Those people who influence our habits have power, even when they are subject to similar manipulations. A man with a bucket of grain can lead a bull to slaughter, but, at least, the oats are objectively real. People can pursue attainable things, such as a new car, a lover or money, or they can chase concepts, pure abstractions that might be untrue. Our ancestors participated in witch burning and human sacrifice, believing that both would afford them some benefit. We have no reason to think that our powers of abstraction are weaker than our forbearers; we have the good fortune of learning from their mistakes. With some luck, future generations will learn from the mistakes that we make today.

Surprise disillusionment can force us to question our beliefs about both the world and ourselves. If we dare enter into the unknown, then we will not be imitating others or relying on habits, as both methods of learning suggest that we know the outcome. Kabir's words point to discovery apart from aping others and repetition based on the past.

Many people may admire Kabir's poetry, but I doubt whether they really see the personal relevance. I chose poems for this book that coincide with the points that I am eager to clarify. Others will certainly derive different meanings from the stanzas, which is why I appeal to experience through everyday examples. If we recognize what Kabir is saying from our own experiences, then that understanding will stand apart from poetic idealism. Our lives are short. Lovers of truth cannot get back time spent separating the worthwhile from the worthless and, often, their efforts lead to disappointment, which is why we should scrutinize any subjective explanations.

Motives are subjective. Discussions about motives include mistakes that come at the expense of misery, but motives remain important. We guess at motives every day when we see advertising or when others suggest a course of action. We constantly make value judgments about both things and people; however, one must wonder whether our judgments are blinded by false beliefs and prejudice. I ask the reader to suspend any verdict until the end of the book. Then, in the spirit of this poet who did not hesitate to criticize, my dear reader, you should scrutinize the views I offer in this book for the love of what is true.

> "No elephant can sift the crystals from the grains. Kabir says,
> renounce all family, caste, and clan. Turn into an ant, instead
> - pick the sugar from the sand and eat."

TWSPP119

I followed Kabir's advice and chose the poems for this book as examples of his best. If you wonder what Kabir might think of me collating his prose with my own explanations, then let the poet speak for himself.

> "He says his, listens to mine; having listened, makes both
> one. I've watched the whole world go by, but haven't found
> such a one."

TBoK PP126

I united up to date examples and observations with Kabir's prose to show how relevant his understanding is today. Writing about people from the past invites error due to the limits of time, rumor and the tendency to appropriate words for purposes other than originally intended. Kabir cannot approve or deny what I am doing. However, he did give counsel.

> "Use the strength of your own arm, stop putting hope in others. When the river flows through your own yard, how can you die of thirst?"

> TBoK PP122

The reader will assign value to this work or withhold it. Too often, others tell us what to respect, rather than encouraging us to respect what is inherently worthy. I encourage the reader to trust the strength of their own judgment without looking to authority.

> "Kabir, sow such a seed that its tree will flourish perennially: cool shade, abundant fruit, foliage full of birds at play."

> TWS PP177

The tree has grown for more than five centuries in spite of idiots having hewn upon it with axes. It did not die. Will we taste the fruit, hear the song and find ease beneath it?

> "A diamond fell in the market, lay in the trash. Many busy fools passed by. A tester took it away."

> TBoK PP109

We can test what we read by referring to our own experience.

The Songs

Poetry suggests a different way of looking at life by describing events and internal experiences with metaphors. A report limited to facts alone would not accomplish the same result. Kabir uses imagination by boldly weaving together emotion, intuition, facts and criticism, while also guiding the way out of imagination into life. We will miss something if we only admire his verses as distant ideals. If we feel dazzled, while musing over a dancing fire, we may discount the power hidden in one glowing cinder. Kabir attacked pretense with flame and any integrity that can survive the ordeal remains intact among the ashes.

When we imagine who we are, we impose limits accordingly. Kabir points to the recognition that our lives include choices beyond the limits that we impose. With luck, disillusionment will reveal the many alternatives available to us before our bodies fall between the mill-stones of death.

"Seeing the mill turn brings tears to the eyes. No one who falls between the stones comes out unbroken."

TBoK PP104

Many of our consoling beliefs become a source of anguish when the real circumstances of life are out-of-sync with our expectations. The facts of life can slap us and shatter our beliefs. If we try changing the way we put on a coat using the secondary arm first, we expose the power of unconscious repetition. Our habits operate blindly and limit the use of our sensitivities and faculties. On the one hand, habits can liberate us from thinking about something redundant. The more a musician unconsciously knows the instrument, the more his mind can explore an abundance of choices in order to create. However, much of life and human interaction are different from playing an instrument with strings and keys always in the same spot. Constantly changing events suggest that we should not seek to live on autopilot. We do not let go of bad habits unconsciously. We cannot make a habit of breaking habits. When we consign a response or belief into a thoughtless mechanical routine, it takes conscious effort to reject it, even if we only want to replace it with a new and better habit. A racist does not have to strain to think the way he does, it happens automatically. To escape bigotry, the racist must consciously choose to do something other than obey the habit.

Belief, right or wrong, affects our behaviors. For example, my father returned late from work after being gone for several days. It was hot despite being quite late. My mother slept while my father disrobed and prepared for bed. He thought to open the sliding glass door opposite the bed to let in some air. As he slid the door open, he heard the faintest noise, in spite of the fact that he was hard of hearing. Being familiar with the sound of a hammer being pulled back on a 357 magnum, he said, "Honey, it's me." Then, my mother, who had been silent until this point, and had almost shot her husband, commenced to give him a piece of her mind in a rant that he did not contest. Take my word for it, my father was as close to dying as one can be and still live. You see, my mom mistook him for an intruder, and a naked one at that. All she saw was the silhouette of a naked man. What we believe matters a lot, especially when it is wrong.

Not everyone is lucky enough to have access to facts that controvert flawed beliefs. Still, when events threaten our viewpoints, we may excuse contrary facts as an exception to the rule and the beliefs stand as strong as before. The more serious the disillusionment, the more difficult it becomes to explain away contradictions. When events of our lives surpass our capacities to rationalize, then our confidence will shatter, particularly regarding beliefs about ourselves. Kabir's poems take the place of disillusioning events to quicken our understanding about life. When we let go of prejudices, we gain access to alternative ways of responding.

If we can avoid misunderstandings by upgrading our language, then we should do so whenever possible. A self-serving pragmatist can twist spiritual terminology to mean anything. Spiritual language desperately calls for improvement and, with this in mind, I occasionally redefine words. For example, I redefined the Sanskrit term *maya*, which typically means illusion or something conjured. When this word maya appears, I ask the reader to treat this word as synonymous with the more precise term *hypothetical*. With this new understanding of *maya*, I can absorb any meaning intended by the former traditional definition. The esoteric word *maya* comes with a lot of superstitious baggage that clouds understanding. The deductive term *hypothetical* frees us from the mumbo jumbo without sacrificing any content.

The Self

In the not so distant future, science may explain human consciousness in completely materialistic terms. The social product of language will be inseparable as part of any explanation. How consciousness exists is not the problem I am interested in,[iv] instead, I am interested in the problem of human misery that arises from identifying ourselves with experiences and ideas. Let us remember that what we mean by consciousness does not come with a label. Any explanation of consciousness (or anything else) must be a product of the mind, a hypothesis.

When our ancestors saw an infection and explained the sickness to be the result of evil spirits, that misguided thesis was as much a product of the mind as Pasture's brilliant germ theory. The differences between the two explanations are that germ theory is far more realistic as it can be tested and lead to better predictions and treatments. Still, germ theory is not made of germs, but rather ideas about germs. The understanding of how ideas represent other things shines a light on what we call identity.

We begin to conceive of ourselves at a young age. We typically embark on a lifelong habit of using a mental schematic of 'I' as a point of reference to solve problems. When, as a child, I wanted candy, my lack of candy was the problem. I tried whining at my mother in the store. When that failed, I put the candy in my pocket without paying for it. Notice the word 'I' in the story. That 'I' represented symbolically what I thought about myself as a complex concept, a fiction. Still, the concept of 'I' in any of our minds, just as in the mind of a child, is no less an object of thought than a belief in evil spirits or germ theory. We have no reason to believe any notion of ourselves must be who we truly are, any more than a mental representation of a banana can satisfy our hunger. Identity is a bundle of thought that we call 'I'. It is an explanation, a symbolic representation.

When we habitually insist that ideas or experiences are evidence, or somehow reflect who we really are, then we are maintaining a mental sense of self. We hold this 'I' as something more than a concept. Nothing conceived can be the object represented. Life forces us beyond the limits of our identities and misery follows when we discover our identities are false. Whatever we attain, no amount of wealth, power, prestige or agreeable circumstances can make a mental self anything more than thought.

The desire to escape the suffering involved in the disillusionment of our identities creates a demand for a solution. When a demand exists, a market usually emerges to supply the desire. The marketplace offers two means by which to solve the problem of identity: material acquisition and spirituality, both of which come in various forms. Materialism strives to create and sustain agreeable circumstances to stabilize a sense of self, while spirituality tries to create or maintain a sense of self that is stable in all circumstances. Most people seem to pursue both methods and favor one over the other based on preference or prejudice. Someone imagines that he will come to rest when he makes his next million (or billion), another imagines respite in heaven, while another envisions the beatitude of enlightenment. Even in hell, there is consolation because the idea of 'I' appears eternal and stable even in imagined eternal misery. Each imagined future includes the idea of a sustained and stable sense of self.

Let us contemplate human aspiration and consider side-by-side, a thrill seeker and someone meditating. In each instance, their methods arrest the day-to-day habits of the mind and cause an out-of-the-ordinary state. The daredevil takes great risks, but the spiritual seeker faces more subtle dangers in the maze of superstitious meaning added to non-typical sensations. The labeling and defining of spiritual experience not only invites spiritual egoism and competition, but, also, creates a struggle to chase better sensations or sustain satisfying experiences. The changing nature of experience renders this effort futile.

It is important to make a distinction between two different types of spiritual seekers. Someone looking for a reflection of themselves in their spiritual experiences is doing something different than someone who quiets the mind without getting lost in the novelty of an altered state. The latter does not seek to prove an idea about the self through experiences that come and go. In moments of silence, we can become conscious of the coming and going activity of the mind, including the bundle of thought that we call self. We realize that the complex object of thought cannot be who we are and the struggle to maintain any such false identity ceases. Please note that an expansion of the topic of self appears at the conclusion of this book in the epilogue.

To avoid confusion, the reader should be aware that Kabir speaks the word 'Brahmin' in two extremely different ways; one is referring to the highest social cast in Indian society, in this context, he is usually being critical. He also uses the word Brahmin in another sense, representing what is best within us all. He uses several terms to suggest consciousness itself i.e. nameless one, Ram, Brahma, Hari, the formless one or silence, he is pointing to the unarticulated, unidentified awareness that remains when the ideas of the self are not present.

Forbidden Subjects

Let us let go of taboos when encountering poems. A lyricist mixes metaphors like a cook making soup. Before you taste this broth, be warned, I like spice! When we allow bold statements, we quickly clarify ideas that might otherwise be obscure, hence the following metaphor. Prostitutes who serve women were once talked about in hushed and disbelieving tones, but a quick internet search of the terms *female sex tourism* shows that these behaviors exist and have their own market. Sex for sale now attracts women with disposable income. The allegory that follows applies to both men and women.

Things happen in brothels beyond the pale of tradition, proving possibilities exist outside of custom. Do you wonder what you are missing? Yet, it is forbidden to go. If you went, what would your mother say? To break the taboo, cowards armor themselves with arrogance and display contempt for women who know their hidden desires. Isn't that why these ladies are condemned by the masses? Kabir knew many secrets and, likewise, suffered derision.

Cowards are often cruel, weak and hide in groups, feeling safer with foolish comrades. They are like thieves ransacking a home without finding the treasure in plain sight. The ignorant take only what they believe to be valuable. Gorging on wine and food, they leave with a night's guilty pleasure, followed by a hangover. They may even speak of disappointment. Do not imitate these pathetic men when entering a brothel or reading a poet.

Kabir's verses are like women at a brothel. Have courage and remove your religious and social prohibitions. After all, if customary correctness were really satisfying, there would be no business for brothels at all. Discard beliefs at the door like uncomfortable secondhand clothes. Now, be honest! You do not go to a brothel to pass the time, for idle conversation or drinks. Why pretend? Why hide your blush? There is no need to be false. The women know exactly why you came. You cannot pretend in front of them. Do not denigrate such women or mimic the hypocrites who will not come in; pretenders who enact both virtue and disdain publicly, while, in their blood, they burn with lust. If you have gathered enough courage to enter, then do not be a coward once you pass the door. Surrender to these women! Many are there and, like poems, a few always stand out. See the one with eyes flashing like lightning in the night sky. She reveals things in a strange way, other than what you have known. Another has strength and can overwhelm you. One more sees your pettiness and contemptuously impugns you with a glance. Yet another has a warmth and kindness that rivals the gift of your own mother's breast.

If you want help understanding Kabir's verses, then take off the clothes that hide your reality. Stop pretending to be anything that you are not and hear his song. The risk of this prose surpasses the charms of the above-mentioned women. Unlike prostitutes, Kabir offers beautiful gifts without charge. He exposes you in a way that does not pass like an evening's delight. Leaving a bordello, you again dress and return to routine. Like a child, you can make-believe that you are something else. However, Kabir seeks to destroy pretense and burn the bridges from the past; he leaves you without a false sense of security. You can dive deeply into one moment and abandon the travails. Now, see what remains.

Enough foreplay!

What do you desire?

Will you give up yourself when the clothes of pretentiousness fall away? Will you yield? Will passion drive you nearer to the beloved, while you whisper "yes"? What if a beautiful lie, to which you were promised, bursts in shrieking, "Stop! I will be anything you want. You cannot possibly want that truth so crass and ugly. It is your duty to remain with me!" In that moment, can you say "No! I desire the beloved that no lie can rival"?

Come! Oh, will you come and meet someone dear. He thought you might be coming and he prepared a gift. Do not be afraid. He is a loving and simple man, a weaver by trade and his name is Kabir.

Desire

> I played for ten years with the girls my own age,
> but now I am suddenly in fear.
> I'm on the way up some stairs - they are high.
> Yet I have to give up my fears
> if I want to take part in this love.
> I have to let go of the protective clothes
> and meet him with the whole length of my body.
> My eyes will have to be the love-candles this time.
> Kabir says: Men and women in love will understand
> this poem.
> If what you feel for the Holy One is not desire,
> then what's the use of dressing with such care,
> and spending so much time making your eyelids
> dark?

TKB PP42

He does not say that spiritual seekers or ascetics will comprehend his meaning, but notes that lovers will. Our poet wants us to have the experience of being in love as a step toward greater liberation. Lovers mistake the dissolving of the ego in orgasm to be only part of orgasm when it results from arresting habits of mind. If we can't let go of our self, orgasm becomes difficult. In the ecstasy of love, the mental specter of our self becomes unsustainable. We live without a story for a few moments. If we need others to see beyond our ideas of ourselves, then possessiveness haunts us. We become a burden to others and limit our choices by reducing people into nothing more than a means. When we use people, we probably destroy or limit our affections in the process. Emancipate others from being just a prop in a cerebral autobiography.

We all walk toward the destruction of delights. With death, we must let go. Lovers in ineffable swoon come close as metaphor. Let us delight in our passions and stoke the desire to understand our alternatives as prejudice lets go. Consciousness exists regardless of the shifting experience. Let go of the fanciful ghost called self.

In the garden the bee lingers;
so many fragrant flowers there.
In the senses the creature lingers;
finally it goes out in despair.

TBoK PP99

Kabir knows the anguish of seeing himself reflected in experience. If we are lost in the pretense, then we spend our time constantly trying to reinforce its reality. We look to our sensations, searching for something that we cannot find. Still we can notice sensations are ephemeral and prone to error. We can know that expecting joy to reinforce our identity is absurd.

What is that flute whose music
thrills me with joy?
The flame burns without a lamp;
The lotus blossoms without a root;
Flowers bloom in clusters;
The moon-bird is devoted to the moon;
With all its heart the rain-bird longs
for the shower of rain;
But upon whose love does the Lover
concentrate His entire life?

SoK PP98

From what source does our love spring and do we really have different types of love, one for parents, another for friends and another for lovers? Could it be that we have one love that takes many different forms, like the ocean having different waves? Who loves when love happens? Something remains when we surrender our minds to love. If we define that consciousness, then we go wrong, for it is more subtle then the tender joys that take place within awareness. It is un-analyzable, at least in current language.

Subtle is the path of love!
Therein there is no asking and
no not-asking,
There one loses one's self at His feet,
There one is immersed in the joy of
the seeking: plunged in the deeps
of love as the fish in the water.
The lover is never slow and offering his
head for his Lord service.
Kabir declares the secret of this love.

SoK PP100

Joy would have less value, if any, if we were not conscious of it. The pursuit of pleasure both admits and introduces us to consciousness. The surrender to ecstasy and letting go of oneself happen together. It is difficult to delight if we are on autopilot. When we see a toddler jumping and laughing, the child is not making a hedge bet or thinking "do I look silly?" The child's happiness is total, a body dancing; the glee is contagious. Adults in a swoon come close; we want to be more in the present. We forget about our routine egocentricity.

Make Your Own Decision.
See for yourself while you live.
Find your own place.
Dead, what house will you have?
Creature, you don't see
your opportunity.
In the end no one belongs to you.
Kabir says, it's difficult,
this wheel of time.

TBoK PP68

In the past, women were not only means, but also personal property. In some countries, morality took a forward step, both men and woman became mutually a means; the usury became more symmetrical. Each person owned a share in the other person. It was quid pro quo; a transaction just like we have with a vendor in a roadside market. However, the consideration is not black and white. When we ask for help, or share the bills or, like myself, ask a beloved to make coffee in the morning, we are using another person. The benefits we share by helping each other are not the problem. When we see others *only* as a way to achieve something, then we are in a prison of selfishness. When another has value beyond what he or she does for us, then his or her life, happiness and choices are precious. These people can say no to us and remain lovable.

Let us consider extreme examples in order to dive deeper into an elusive distinction between means and ends.

Richard and Mavis were married for about 50 years. They lived and worked together in a successful business. I was acquainted with these affable people because Rich worked on my grandfather's agricultural equipment. Rich decided to end his own life after an accident where a large piece of machinery fell and left him crippled and in pain. Before shooting himself, he shot his wife several times through a bathroom door. She survived this nightmare and he did not. Contrast this situation with an account from *The Gulag Archipelago*, where Solzhenitsyn described the torture of political prisoners under Stalin. Some of these victims were rare people who were willing to be tortured to death without breaking; these people would often surrender their wills when Soviet officials would bring in their families and threaten them with agony and death.

There are many possible interpretations of the above cases about people in severe pain, nearing death. Yet, there is a vast difference between the two. In one case, the life of Mavis appeared to have no value outside of the purpose Rich assumed she served. In the other, not only the lives, but also the well-being of the family had more value than both the prisoner's life and the ideals for which the prisoner was willing to die. With these few unique prisoners, the family had inherent value as ends unto themselves.

Most of us probably feel insulted when others use us only as a means. This situation frequently happens in the interaction between corporations and consumers. In America, sick people must often fight with insurance companies to pay legitimate claims. The fraudulent administrative tactics are routine and performed by everyday working people on others like themselves. In these instances, employees surrender judgment to superiors and abandon personal responsibility. The victims of this clerical sleight of hand are only a means for profit. What is more surprising is that we can *value ourselves only as a means*. We may imagine some result is more important than our life to the point that we are willing to risk our life to achieve it. What is tragic is that the ideal sought may be an unattainable fiction.

When we hazard an elective operation like breast implantation, we are imagining a future benefit. Still, voluntary patients are willing to wager risks to their lives for the sake of a vain ideal. Occasionally, complications from surgery prove fatal, but let's call attention to the higher levels of suicide in women with breast implants. Any explanation of this fact would be impossible to prove. Regardless, we should not dismiss the possibility that these people concluded that their lives had little or no value when they did not achieve the results that they sought. Whether you agree with my explanation of these tragedies, one thing seems undeniable, the beliefs upon which our value judgments rest are not frivolous matters and Kabir is clear on this point. Do not to defer to others.

> **There is a strange tree, which**
> **stands without roots and bears**
> **fruits without blossoming;**
> **It has no branches and no leaves, it is**
> **lotus all over.**
> **Two birds sing there; one is the guru,**

<blockquote>
and the other the disciple:
The disciple chooses the manifold fruits
of life and tastes them, and the
guru beholds him in joy.
What Kabir says is hard to understand:
"the bird is beyond seeking, yet it
is most clearly visible. The form-
less is in the midst of all forms. I
sing the glory of forms."
</blockquote>

SoK PP94

Above, Kabir treats both the guru and disciple as equals. Remember that human life is not an incarnation of something divine, but an incarnation of matter becoming aware. Our desires can be in conflict with the truth when facts run contrary to our wants. When conflicts of motives arise, we can value the facts or we sometimes pretend that the facts are different. We feel a temptation and change the meaning of circumstances according to our desires. Such delusion is the enemy of integrity. Kabir reminds us not to fall into the terror of losing something we desire.

<blockquote>
Seeing gold and sexy bodies,
don't be dazed by the colors.
Meeting, parting-trivial,
like a skin dropped by a snake.
</blockquote>

TBoK PP106

When others seem more fortunate than ourselves, we subject our emotions to the power of imagination. Ideas about others become a cage when we compare ourselves to them; do not walk into that trap. We can go beyond both acquisition and renunciation and see through the beliefs about what we must have or what we must surrender in order to have a valid life. The ideas in our mind about other people are not who they truly are. When we compare a fiction about ourselves to the fiction that we have created about others, we create misery. Do not give possessions more importance than they deserve and remember that they are temporary. Let us put a check on imagining that a wonderful state will compensate us for the sacrifices necessary to achieve it. That idea can be terribly wrong and we will not get back any time lost.

> **Dance, my heart! Dance to-day**
> **with joy.**
> **The strains of love fill the days and**
> **the nights with music, and the**
> **world is listening to its melodies:**
> **Mad with joy, life and death dance to**
> **the rhythm of this music. The**
> **hills and the sea and the earth**
> **dance. The world of man dances**
> **in laughter and tears.**
> **Why put on the robe of the monk, and**
> **live aloof from the world in lonely**
> **pride? Behold! My heart dances in the delight of a hundred arts;**
> **and the**
> **Creator is well pleased.**

SoK PP80

No reason exists to be detached from the world, as if that were even possible. The pleasure of a beloved and the tears when they depart are part of living. Kabir is not just lukewarm in loving. He isn't separating the pleasures of love from the tears in order to keep only what he prefers. What begins eventually, passes away, so now is the time to enjoy!

Take the heavens, utopias and ideals of happily ever after that people have never achieved, include the ones for which people were willing to die. If we throw these perfections on one side of a scale and, on the other side, put a live hummingbird egg, which weighs more? My point is that *this life* is not an ideal. It exists in the ordinary workaday world where the action really happens. Anyone who thinks facts are not sacred has not fully grasped the power of a fact to destroy illusion. We may try something new imagining a better outcome; this action is the foundation of progress. We account for the results and our success or failure will be factual. When we fail, remember these disappointments are the strains, they are part of the rhythm of life.

"The *sentimentalist fallacy* is to shed tears over abstract justice and generosity, beauty, etc., and never to know these qualities when you meet them in the street." [v]

William James

I am acquainted with a man who, as a teenager, received such a horrible beating while in police custody that he lost his front teeth. The officers let him go free to avoid any consequences for their actions. As he walked down the road in a dreadfully bloody state, a woman pulled over and let him in her car. Seeing his situation, she felt moved to take him to a dentist. She paid the bills to repair the damage and for dentures without asking anything in return. We cannot separate the charity of this woman from the vulgarity of the circumstance. Some members of our human family were born into brutal suffering and they have known little else. In such a case, a pessimistic worldview is understandable, but that does not make that belief true. If we understand that there is more to the world and ourselves then our beliefs about either, we gain access to choices that our beliefs would never allow.

Let go the idealism that hopes for joy apart from sadness. Kabir's poetry embraces realism, including unwanted events. A difference exists between trying something new and deeming the world as it is to be contemptible. One effort tries to discover something better and the other pessimistically rejects what life has to offer. To treat everything as trash because it is not idyllic assumes not only to know all that the world can ever possibly offer, but also the wisdom to judge all of those events and find them lacking before they happen. That is quite arrogant.

> **A gown of love-silk -**
> **put it on, Kabir,**
> **and dance!**
> **They shine with beauty**
> **who speak truth**
> **with mind and body.**

TBoK PP95

Delusion can just as easily undervalue pleasure as it can overestimate its importance. If we want sex and pretend otherwise, then there is no honesty. If we have little or no interest in sex and make believe the opposite, then we are equally deceitful.

Hidden in this everyday world are things of great value that we miss if we limit ourselves to a cunning façade. There are two treasures often hidden in our own lives, one is the recognition of our joy and the second is the recognition of what we cannot accomplish through the satisfaction of desire. When we stop expecting our delights to achieve some other ideal, then we find ourselves without as many disappointments. Such a loss of misery is a great gain.

> **In Maya's flames the world burns,**
> **burns for gold and sex.**
> **Kabir says, how to save it**
> **when the fire is swathed in cotton?**

TBoK PP106

In our minds, we can create a future along with an imagined self, in a fictional story about the world. We wear this narrative like combustible swaddling clothes. People around us will stoke our fires of avarice, especially those individuals who have something to sell. Our dreams of wealth, power and pleasure in some tomorrow devour many possibilities today. Consider those of us who are so greedy that they conceive of unending satisfaction after death. That is what heaven is, a state of unending contentment of utterly satisfied desires. Some people deny themselves pleasure that can be quite harmless in order to purchase a heaven beyond life. We need not spend the gap between diapers and the grave measuring the value of our lives by what we do not have. Let us not bond ourselves to a master called more.

The motives that drive people toward delusions are neither new nor specific to a particular group. I give special attention to my compatriots who, on the whole, suffer terribly from this affliction called *more*. My American brothers and sisters, you know bloody fucking well I am talking about you.

Who will be sheriff
in a town littered with meat
where the watchmen
is a vulture?
Mouse in the boat,
cat at the oars;
frog sleeping,
snake on guard;
bull giving birth,
cow sterile,
calf milked morning, noon and night;
lion forever leaping
to fight the jackal.
Kabir says, rare listeners
hear the song right.

TBoK PP73

My beloved Sharon has shared a friendship with another woman for over 35 years. The remarkable sexual escapades of this unnamed (still living) woman are notorious among those who know her. In the early 1970s, she became offended by the moral ministering of the lofty preachers of several local churches. She responded by fucking each one of them. She wanted to see first-hand if their moral reality coincided with their words, and they did not. She still feels some guilt about this action today. She mentioned that only one of the many men put up any resistance at all. She responded by going regularly on Sunday to his sermons and beaming at him from the front pew with longing looks of admiration. Before long, she subjected him to her charms as well. Such a woman can expose a thousand hypocrites in as many days. If you imagine her to be a stunning beauty, you would be wrong. Her common looks lacked those curves that men value so highly. Yet, her vivacity and real interest in sex gave her power. However, the pleasure that comes with command over men does not give security.

From the time girls become aware of the differences between the sexes they watch many men take women for granted. Men ignore, deceive and often discard women, especially when they age; like a peel after consuming the fruit. It seems the same fate quite possibly awaits them unless they become predatory. Some women decide it is better to use than to be used. This decision is called being *smart*. We often see the same attitude in business.

When the inclination to see others only as a means becomes a trend, it is not so easy to distinguish between cats and mice. Then, kindness becomes mistaken for weakness and strength gets confused with cruelty. In this tragically common situation, we may curb affections for the sake of outcomes that exist in fantasy.

Kabir dances, sings and knows the joys of life and love. Why is he so terse with people, so critical? He is not condemning the pleasures of life, but our beliefs about them and what we think satiety would do for us. The search for more plagues us, while we cling to the idea of how things ought to be. Someone thinks, "If 'I' had that lover, if 'I' were beautiful, if 'I' had more money or if 'I' were enlightened, then 'I' would be content." We know the limits of gratification; they are obvious from the satisfaction of past desires. Lovers seem to be the most precious treasures, especially when out of our reach. Nevertheless, when we imagine we possess them, we taint the love with our expectations because no matter how good the lovers are, they cannot do for us what we demand. We even resent them for coming up short. The same holds for owning objects. The hourglass drains, while we waste our time believing the superstitions about contented wants.

We call our impulses by many names: such as joy, desire, competition, pride, love of power, anger, ambition, fear and, even, misery. These motives cheat us because we cannot hold on to anything we might achieve, not even pain. In a moment of satisfaction, we live without hankering. A fleeting experience can point the way to understanding or become an entrance to a vicious circle. Satiety eludes us, so we are tempted to seek another goal. More insidiously, we conjure up what it means about ourselves if we do not get what we want; our lives seem futile and we are unworthy. Good salespersons know this secret. This fiction becomes motivation if we mistake it for a reflection of who we are as it makes us slaves to our cravings.

> **The mind dwells in front of the eyes**
> **and runs with every blink.**
> **In the three worlds mind is king.**
> **Everyone worships the mind.**

TBoK PP118

Our poet seems unequivocal when he says "everyone worships the mind." What does he mean? All of the gods, religions and our egos we build out of ideas. If we dismiss Kabir's warning, then we do so at our own cost. We frequently take our interpretations for granted and as a result, do not distinguish between our ideas and things. Delusion, deliberation and, even, contemplation of what is true can be confused because all have mind in common. If a belief can alter the interpretation of our senses, then the results can vary. One belief that occupies a large portion of our experience, but frequently goes unaccounted for, is the concept of self. These ideas of 'I' act as a fulcrum for our judgments about the world. If we reflect on the beliefs that our ancestors held as part of some now dead religion, we wonder how these people could guide their lives and judgments based on beliefs that seem to us to be absurd. Do we also currently possess the same weakness as our ancestors for believing in the absurd? I think the answer to this question is yes; the difference is that our superstitions have become more sophisticated.

> **O Yogi,**
> **the world of Maya**
> **is hard to renounce.**
> **When I renounced my home,**
> **I was trapped in my clothes;**
> **when I renounced my clothes,**
> **I was stuck with my mendicants rounds.**
> **When I renounced desire,**
> **anger wouldn't leave me;**
> **when I renounced anger,**
> **I was stuck with greed.**
> **When I renounced greed,**
> **my ego wouldn't leave me –**
> **my self regard, my boastfulness,**
> **my attachment to appearances.**
> **When my mind was finally detached,**
> **I renounced the whole world of Maya:**
> **my concentration, my ancient memory,**
> **then fused with my words.**
> **Kabir says, listen,**
> **my good brothers -**
> **one in a million**
> **has solved this mystery**

TWS PP198

Nakedly showing his past mistakes, Kabir speaks to those people around him who knew both indulgence and renunciation. Many teachings advocate repressing desire in pursuit of ideals. Then, believers seek obscure loopholes in their beliefs in order to indulge in forbidden fruits. Women accused of immorality in orthodox cultures are shamed, beaten, groped, raped and, even, killed by fanatics pointing at religious justifications. Such gross rationalizations for anger and lust continue even as believers condemn the violence, but cower before challenging the beliefs. The moderates seem almost invisible behind those individuals who compel attention with radical and, often, violent behavior.

Even the disciplines we impose on ourselves for the sake of a better life cannot escape scrutiny. An athlete pushes himself in painful ways in order to achieve a better result. A spiritual seeker, like a farmer with an orchard, prunes his desires to achieve a better result. The appearance of discipline disguises ambition behind colorful ornaments. Spiritual practices are, in general, merely a means to some imagined end. Whether or not the results we seek are attainable is a different question.

Our beliefs are not true, although some are arguably better adapted to given circumstances than others, and many look false upon closer inspection. Let's treat mind constructs as best guesses at reproducing our world. Instead of renouncing the world as an illusion, which treats the illusion as something real (Why renounce what doesn't exist?), let us, instead, see our thought forms as what they are, a mental model of the world that can be improved.

A parent considering what his child is doing when out of sight, a lover contemplating the beloved and any considerations about ourselves have some things in common. They reference past experiences, interpret those experiences through beliefs and combine this information into a vague representation in the mind. At best, these things are approximations. It is common to find out that the representation is flawed or even wrong. We are not compelled to believe or obey these mental constructs if we understand that they are objects of thought.

> Swan, you're strong
> but your habits are weak.
> You're streaked with dirty colors
> and screwing with various lovers.
>
> TBoK PP91

The word *excessive* means something when talking of salt, sex or any experience. Even water will kill you if you drink too much. When we believe some experience or possession will do something it cannot, before we give up the belief, we are likely to see if *more* will accomplish the desired effect. Our beliefs make us vulnerable to hawkers that pander to our desires. Advertisers will sell us anything by suggesting an enviable 'lifestyle' associated with their products. If we look at the *hopes* encouraged in the schemes that promise to help us *become the people we were meant to be*, then we see what we are buying is an image of ourselves in the future that exists in our mind. It is the same for beauty products and soda pop. It is not just that Pepsi is a tasty, sweet drink, the consumers symbolize the *Pepsi generation*, whatever the fuck that means. Advertising infers that happiness results from purchases. Are we victims of another's fraud or our own? I think both. Our part of the fraud remains hidden as long as we wish to judge ourselves based on experiences or possessions.

> Pandit, you've got it wrong.
> There is no creator or creation there,
> no gross or fine, no wind or fire,
> no sun, moon, earth or water,
> no radiant form, no time there,
> no word, no flesh, no faith,
> no cause-and-effect, nor any thought
> of the Veda. No Hari or Brahma,
> no Shiva or Shakti, no pilgrimage
> and no rituals. No mother, father
> or guru there. Is it two or one?

**Kabir says, if you understand now,
you're guru, I'm disciple.**

TBoK PP56

Kabir shows apt humility. If you can reconcile the paradoxes where he cannot, then, without hesitation, he acknowledges your preeminence. Here there are seeming inconsistencies with other of his poems. The weaver risks a refutation out of his own mouth because, in other poems, he references a creator and, above, he says that both the creator and creation do not exist. Admittedly, this is the license of the poet. This inconsistency Kabir accounts for when, later, our poet discusses the limits of all language particularly when discussing subjective states, For example, he says "his creatures have invented these fictions." If we treat knowledge as hypothetical, the door is always open to another saying something better. Kabir refers above to the timeless quiet mind in which we abide without any gods or worship. The quiet mind points to consciousness where the sense of ourselves appears and disappears, but regardless we remain intact. A problem erupts with trying to represent or give a label to unarticulated awareness. Remember that no map perfectly represents the way, but with this flaw admitted, a diagram can still be good enough to get us where we need to go. Unlike the rigid parrots of dogma, our poet says let the representations be improved and may there be gratitude for any innovation.

Kabir could see people lost in their own minds and tried to help. We still face this threat and its dire consequences today. We are not obligated to take thought to be anything but symbolic. We need not fear the mind when, in one stroke, beliefs are rendered nothing more than the countless ideas that flow through our minds daily of which we take little or no account.

**Joy is brief.
Sorrow and grief are endless.
The minds an elephant,**

mad, amnesiac.
Air and flame burns as one,
just as when the moth, its eye enchanted by light,
flies straight into the lamp,
and wing and fire flair together.
Who hasn't found
restful peace in a moment of pleasure?
So you brush aside the truth,
and chase the lies you hold so dear.
At the end of your days
you feel the temptation, you covet joy,
even though old age and death
are close at hand.
The world's embroiled in illusion, error:
this is the process always in motion.
Man attains a human birth:
why does he waste and destroy it?

TWS PP151

Believing appealing ideas requires little effort. Just think of the centuries past and the beliefs held in superstitions that a fool would now reject. Can we even count the lives lost because of credulity? We have reason to suspect that we too can believe falsehoods just as our ancestors did. The fictions that appeal to us may be different, but that does not change the realities of life that we must deal with as facts.

Centuries before Viagra exposed the carnal desires of our contemporary elders, a poem divulged the same yearning. Throughout time, many with grey hair have done things that might astound the young. Some lusty women in retirement communities keep liquor on hand just in case some able-bodied man wants a drink. If you have doubts about what I say, and you possess a little courage, volunteer in a retirement community. However, the curious should beware, comforting illusions about older people evaporate easily and you will probably understand how retirees in America are spreading so much venereal disease.

It's plain our opportunities for pain may well outnumber the occasions for delight, but I must criticize either the poet or translator. In imagination only, misery seems eternal, but grief and sorrow are not endless or reliable. Death will snatch away both agony, and joy. We have many opportunities to feel pain in life, we need not add to that fact by creating torments and ghosts in our mind to haunt us. When despair and avoiding pain become a preoccupation; we forget that our experiences come and go.

Do people seek enjoyment for its own sake, use it as a painkiller or use it for another purpose? Our diversions come and go like the tide and offer no reliable refuge. Kabir knows about seeking "peace in a moment of pleasure" because he has sought it. The ease in such moments lulls us into daydreams. The warning against illusion shines clear. Do not forget the past failures to achieve security through indulgence; we end up running after the next desire as our life drains away. We can even create misery, while we will seek more pleasure.

Delectable food, wine, drugs, leisure diversions, sex, beauty, wealth, glory, righteousness and power are all temporary. The credulous are taught that holy versions of these delights are permanent in exchange for doing "good." Ironically, many of those individuals who profit from these bargains use their gains to enjoy pleasures. When we mistake experience for evidence of "who we are," then we become worshipers of sensuality and wish for permanent satisfaction. This demand has created a market filled with religion and superstition.

The best of all true things

is a true heart.

Without truth no happiness,

though you try

a million tricks.

TBoK PP95

We see people profiting from deceit as a means to their desired ends. To assert that "without truth no happiness," seems to go too far, but does it? The exploiter lives in fear of reprisal. Those individuals who indulge in distortions must also hide from the truth. When facts expose a lie, then the house of cards must fall. Ruthless kings employed people to taste their food for poison. Despots suspect their underlings of treachery. Shall we call this true happiness? I do not think so.

Let us distinguish sincerity from integrity. A person can sincerely devote his life to a false belief and he can kill or die for it. One with integrity would rather be in the unknown than credit doubtful beliefs or deceive others. Uprightness belongs to those individuals who are willing to doubt. Integrity includes more than a misgiving about the ideas of others; it must also include misgivings about our own ideas. When our beliefs exclude relevant facts, those beliefs are at least flawed and perhaps false.

We can stop flattering any self that we invent and cease relying on groups where stated agreement grants membership and prestige. Our guardians dress us in identities like costumes. We become white collar or blue collar. We become Americans or Canadians. We become Christian, Muslim or Hindu. No one reads scripture in the womb. We are not born as any of these things and we don't come into life with an idea of racial or class superiority. The more we limit ourselves to the scope of a manufactured identity, the more automatic we become toward life. The habitual pessimist is as much an automaton as the habitual optimist. Our expectations need not be a looking glass through which we judge the world. We come into life and put on beliefs like clothes. Let us not impose baseless limits on the gift of life by surrendering to pretentious and arbitrary labels. If our culture branded us with beliefs like cattle, we still are not bound to obey those beliefs.

The flute of the Infinite is played
without ceasing, and it sound is

love:
when love renounces all limits, it
reaches truth.
How widely the fragrance spreads! It
has no end, nothing stands in its
way.
The form of this melody is bright like
a million suns: incomparably
sounds the vina, the vina of the
notes of truth.

SoK PP96

Who do you know who does not place a boundary around his love? We are afraid others will use us and that our desire for love makes us foolish. In deference to this fear, we try to be smart and use others in the name of love for our own ends. We become what we fear and keep things hidden from our mates, especially the secrets that would show our real thoughts and behaviors. Then, we imagine what it would be like to have real love. Ironically, we dream about what reality would be like if things were different! Inexplicably, we take this dreaming for granted.

If my heart were truly open, then [insert wishful-thinking here].

If that person loved me, then [insert ego-fulfillment here].

We distort our capacity to love others with references to an imaginary future. We see ourselves in this story and believe that we know what love will or should do for us. We use emotion to force others to do what we desire. We even withhold and limit love as a threat, ignoring the fact that death stalks us. If we are stingy with love, then we are drowning in our minds' reflecting pools. We may justify our selfish actions by imagining a resulting love that will exceed the bounds that we impose today! We twist love, confusing it with ego fulfillment.

If our lovers act contrary to our visions, then our self-seeking schemes become more obvious.

A mental sense of self is fiction. Do not insist that we can judge well from such a vapid thing. Others do not exist to prove what we think of ourselves. When we stop mistaking a concept for who we are, we stop demanding that others must sustain our imagined self.

> **Friend, hope for the guest while you are alive.**
> **Jump into experience while you're alive!**
> **Think ... and think ... while you are alive.**
> **What you call "salvation" belongs to the time before death.**
> **If you don't break your ropes while you're alive,**
> **do you think**
> **ghosts will do it after?**
> **The idea that the soul will join with the ecstatic**
> **just because the body is rotten –**
> **that is all fantasy.**
> **What is found now is found then.**
> **If you find nothing now,**
> **you will simply end up with an apartment in the City**
> **of Death.**
> **If you make love with the divine now, in the next life**
> **you will have the face of satisfied desire.**
> **So plunge into the truth,**
> **find out who the Teacher is,**
> **believe in the great sound.**
> **Kabir says this: When the Guest is being searched for,**
> **It is the intensity of the longing for the Guest that**
> **Does all the work**
> **Look at me, and you will see a slave of that intensity.**

TKB PP24

The great sound is the silent awareness behind any hearing. Our consciousness remains open to any experience. We demonstrate our emancipation from beliefs by not being bound to them. If we consciously adapt to life, then we embody what the word *choice* attempts to convey. Having denied the existence of an afterlife repeatedly, Kabir entreats us not to miss the life entrusted to our care. He warns us of a tragic loss that happens more often than not when fantasy replaces the unknown.

> **If you know you're alive,**
> **find the essence of life.**
> **Life is the sort of guest**
> **you don't meet twice.**

TBoK PP90

Those individuals who only lead us into idealism and away from the conditions around us are enemies of clarity, regardless of their good intentions. Chasing after what we can never have, we lose what we can never regain, life itself, which, here, is Kabir's guest and he implores us to treat it with respect.

Mind

> The woman who is separated from her lover
> spins at the spinning wheel.
> The Baghdad of the body rises with its towers and
> gates.
> Inside the palace of intelligence has been built.
> The wheel of ecstatic love turns around in the sky,
> and the spinning seat is made of the sapphires of
> work and study.
> This woman weaves threads that are subtle,
> and the intensity of her praise makes them fine!
> Kabir says I am that woman.
> I am weaving the linen of night and day.
> When my lover comes and I feel his feet,
> the gift I will have for him is tears.

TKB PP59

Kabir uses his intimate knowledge of weaving as a metaphor for the manufacture of ideas. The mind spins a narrative of our life like a spinning wheel makes thread. Remember what we imagined about ourselves a few years ago and how we viewed the world. It's amazing how ridiculous many of those ideas seem today, regardless of how important they seemed at the time. The trifles of our pasts probably seem apparent, but what is not obvious is that we do the same thing today. What reason do we have to expect our current conclusions to be more reliable than in the past? After all, our new conclusions will still be mental objects and subject to our limits and biases. Meaning is something we add to circumstances and it can get us into horrible trouble.

People become lost in the mind because they are not making a distinction between events in life and thoughts about those circumstances, perhaps even going beyond distortions of fact to imagining things that never happened. Our powers of abstraction often work habitually, like the way we maintain racial and sexual stereotypes. When we perceive people, places, and things as props in our mental narrative, we forget how much of the story we create based on our habitual ideas.

The separation that Kabir speaks of is the separation from our life by being fixated on the concept of self. The awareness behind our identity is vague, clouded by thoughts. In the absence of thought, the phantom identity disappears. If we miss this fact, then the ghost of ego will demand a constant effort in order to maintain it.

**"The Baghdad of the body rises with its towers and gates.
Inside the palace of intelligence has been built."**

TKB PP59

The woman's imagination is the artist and she creates a world in her mind. Like her, we can think and provoke strong emotions in ourselves that might be relevant or have little or nothing to do with our lives. Like a puppy following a child, our emotions chase thoughts. This ability to conceive suggests how both our ancestors and contemporaries created gods. We manufacture in mind a powerful *doer* and through their agency, we explain away many unknown things. In a moment without thought, the idea of any god disappears.

We live in the world regardless of our various thoughts about it. We view the world, but life has no obligation to coincide with our ideas. We are like painters, our minds are the canvases, our thoughts are the paint and our desires are the brushes. The artist becomes so fascinated that he loses himself in the world that he creates. We not only learn to induce feelings in ourselves this way, but we also imitate others who do the same, particularly if they have (or seem to have) more success in their lives. How can a Christian, having never met Jesus, believe that he or she has a personal relationship with him? How does anyone presume to know about any heaven? The fear and grief around death reveals the make-believe. Why lament death if you believe that you will meet your beloved in some spiritual Disneyland beyond the grave? People devote a great deal of their lives to trying to enter such an imaginary place and theologians should be ashamed of trying to take advantage of fear and credulity.

"This woman weaves threads that are subtle, and the intensity of her praise makes them fine!"

TKB PP59

Kabir does not mean that subtlety is beautiful, but, rather, that the woman's passion manufactures the beauty. We believe that certain things will make us happy and these ideas emotionally charge our hopes. Consider the adolescent imagining bliss in the arms of a beloved. Conceiving of love when it is not true creates happiness (or the hope for it) that will endure until disillusionment comes.

We admire many concepts not because they are worthy but because we were told they are respectable. These habits of mind may appear harmlessly self-satisfying, but such expectations often become a justification for unrestrained ambition, rivalry, lust for power and fear; these motives, when acted upon, have real world consequences.

"Kabir says I am that woman. I am weaving the linen of night and day."

TKB PP59

Kabir makes no claim to be superior or special. He knows what it is like to fall victim to the seductions of the mind. He knows the beauty and horror that the mind can create and he invites us to avoid the pitfalls of mind. With words, he tries to shake us out of a daydream and opens our eyes to the many alternatives in life that we have been missing while fantasizing. Do not create despair trying to satisfy an ego that we cannot even find. We have the power to spin both night and day, a fictional realm where the ego seems real.

In a moment without thought, the demanding self disappears, leaving us with real limits, but not the fickle restrictions of an imaginary self. Our identity emerges and falls within the quiescence that any thought arises from, like waves on water. This understanding is easy to miss. Meditation is diving into the neutrality of our being. The various forms of introspection are vulnerable to the contamination of wishful thinking. Unfortunately, people mistake meditation as a means to attain some imagined state. Con artists make use of the altered states generated in meditation as proof of their nonsense. We will not gain anything from silence and, instead, will temporarily lose what we build out of thought.

"When my lover comes and I feel his feet, the gift I will have for him is tears."

TKB PP59

The beloved in the poem shows the woman that her identity is not real. The woman at the spinning wheel can stop believing the fictions and avoid the pain of disillusionment. The end of the subjection to our habits of the mind brings tears of gratitude. Thankfulness is not the goal of self-inquiry, but a result of ending the useless creation of suffering; it feels good to get off a bed of thorns. In the quietness behind our thoughts, the ego dissolves along with the world we created in mind for our imagined self, and we still continue to exist. Kabir points toward an understanding of the mind that allows creativity without the burden of identifying ourselves with what we create. Quiet the mind, see the fictions and live.

Long ago in India,[vi] two young men decided to travel together and seek fortune away from their rural village. On their journey, one of the friends died accidentally. One day, the surviving man met a wanderer who mentioned that he would be passing through the hometown of the two adventurous friends. The survivor asked the traveler to relate two messages, one to the family of his deceased friend informing them of the loss and one to his own family telling of his success. He also asked the drifter to tell his family that he intended to return soon with enough money to give them a better life. The drifter agreed. In the course of his travel, the wanderer confused the names, telling the family of the dead man of his good fortune. To the kin of the living, he told of the accidental death. The wrong family rejoiced, while the other bore the pain of sorrow.

We ought to notice from the above tale that something untrue can as easily produce joy as misery. Once we understand this point, it becomes a challenge to any system of thought, religious, therapeutic, intuitive or rational. No philosophy that uses the happiness of its believers as proof that the belief is true can hope to stand unless it accounts for happiness that rests upon what is untrue.

Let us include in our inquiry three mind qualities often discussed in Hinduism, that of sensuality, purity (true knowledge) and delusion. People who believe themselves to be pure or moral, reference a judgment about what is good to prove their identity. Such beliefs are often not devotions to the truth, but to a conceptual sense of self. Many beliefs are complex and contain things that are true and things that are false. It is no wonder that many belief systems reject scrutiny. We must discriminate to avoid throwing out the baby with the bathwater. It sometimes surprises us to find how many beliefs, including those that presume to be holistic, reject reasoning. It is blithe to think any belief system whole if, in order to accept it, we must omit reasoning from the wholeness!

Someone who can show us the weakness in our beliefs may fail to convince us, but the memory will haunt us. Kabir notes that death will emancipate even the most ardent believer, but life can do it, too. It is better if we shake the house of cards that represents our beliefs, than to allow the winds of life to do it.

Consider how sycophantic entourages often surround prestigious people for a share in the glory. The material seekers who cling to others possessing power or wealth often come away with something material for their efforts. In spiritual circles, there are enticements held out as a reward for spiritual practice. The observance of devotions may be little more than temporarily altering ones state and the pursuit of ego fulfillment. When a spiritual seeker finds little or diminishing gratification in return for subjugating themselves, then resentment erupts. When a man does not receive what he bargained for, then he feels angry with the salesman. Sometimes, the dissatisfaction with materialism or spirituality emerges with the approach of death. People may have spent years chasing a mirage. Regardless of choosing a material or spiritual path, similar disillusionment awaits any fictitious sense of self. The aforementioned disenchantments have little to do with inquiry into what is true. Yet, disillusionment may provoke the desire to be free of false beliefs, at which point integrity begins to blossom.

> **Maya's the super swindler.**
> **Trailing the noose of three qualities,**
> **she wonders, whispering**
> **honeyed words.**
> **For Vishnu she's Lakshmi,**
> **for Shiva she's Shakti,**
> **for priests an idol,**
> **for pilgrims a river.**
> **To a monk she's a nun,**
> **to a king she's a queen,**
> **in one house a jewel,**
> **in one a shell.**
> **For devotee's she's a pious lady,**

for Brahma, Mrs. Brahma.
Kabir says, seekers,
listen well:
this is a story
no one can tell.

TBoK PP60

When we treat objects or experiences as proof of who we are, that belief rests on a lie that is hard to see. For some, it is a house, car, money or spouse. If we look a little closer, we may see our identity hiding in everyday things, like a ring on our finger. How well our children do in school becomes evidence of who we are. We tend to add a great deal of meaning to rituals like marriage. The added meaning is often a false sense of security that comes with faith in a familiar belief.

Many dangerous things can hide in what seems inconspicuous. Consider that a platoon of soldiers does not need to look like the surroundings for camouflage to work; they only need to look like something other than armed men. The soldiers' deception works well because they help people see what they prefer to see. Nobody wants to see warriors bringing death. The time needed to escape the combatants or defend against them wastes until the fact of an attack makes it impossible to deny the danger. Now consider how talk of morality lulled countless parents into trusting their children to the care of priests, some of whom were rapists camouflaged in pious robes. The predatory priests helped people to see what they wanted to see. The faithful supplied the predators with both victims and donations that not only maintained the criminals, but undoubtedly helped pay the perpetrators legal fees. I suggest that the parents were chasing both security and identity in their beliefs.

I married my Lord, and meant to live with him.
But I did not live with him, I turned away,
and all it once my twenties were gone.
The night I was married all my friends sang for me,

**and the rice of pleasure and the rice of pain fell
on me.
Yet when all those ceremonies were over, I left, I did
not go home with him,
and my relatives all the way home said,
"It's all right."
Kabir says: Now my love energy is actually mine.
This time I will take it with me when I go,
and outside his house I will blow the horn of
triumph!**

TKB PP43

We ask ourselves variations of the question, "Why do 'I' not feel happiness after doing what 'I' learned to do to have that result?" The people around us with similar beliefs will probably excuse or explain away failures. We tend to condone the roles we play to get by in the world; we play ritual parts in business and even when attracting a lover. Still, the consequences of our actions are our personal responsibilities. If we remain restless, then we may try on a new belief. In spite of some differences or even improvements, we may find more disappointments in different circumstances. We lose our way in the fog of beliefs and, suddenly, our youth is gone. It is not a theoretical question. Many husbands and wives aspire to great love or success and end up resenting the time spent in vain. Some try several times with different partners. In such circumstances, people often confuse being conciliatory with maturity. Couples often vacation together, enjoy dinners, wine, movies, and smile at their partners, while they both rot. We mix our sincere actions with pretensions and what is untrue taints the rest. Whether we enter into a select group, take religious vows or get married, we tend to forget the make-believe and think that the parts we play are our own.

Kabir encourages us to stop blindly following the magisterial beliefs of people we learned to admire as they, in turn, ape others. We can drop the arbitrary roles and allow our affections to arise in response to the events and people around us. We need not withhold love in exchange for others conforming to our ideas. Our love is finally our own.

> **O Kabir, I'm worse than everyone else,**
> **everyone's a better person than me:**
> **anyone who comprehends this**
> **is a dear friend of mine.**

TWS PP178

Identity plays the lead when kneeling in prayer, for without this ego, the god(s) and enlightenment become irrelevant. When people display their ignorance, one who is outside the folly is grateful for being different. The prejudice that Kabir suffered also proved that others were capable of recognizing a difference between Kabir and themselves. The poet values the seed of discernment in his detractors, it is an opportunity; the germ might sprout at any moment. These insolent ones are only lacking a correct judgment of value. His detractors are one step away from a profound recognition. Kabir implies it is better to be different then be on autopilot, even if it means that others will look upon you with scorn. This poet also knew the disapproval of a fool is its own kind of complement. We have learned to grant merit to those individuals of higher class, those individuals who possess power and those on spiritual paths, but Kabir says no! They, too, chase the mirage by envisioning their future in this life or beyond. They seek to derive security from things that they can and will eventually lose, including a God that loves them. These people trust a daydream. Self-obsession hides in both the mundane and sacred. The real object of affection is the self, regardless of the material or spiritual ornaments we hide that ego behind.

> **So what if you drop illusion?**
> **You didn't drop your pride.**
> **Pride has fooled the best sages,**
> **pride devours all.**

TBoK PP106

Let us assume an identity superior to that of an average person through wealth, prestige or accomplishment. The merits of such a person would not make his sense of self more substantial than the thought that composes anyone else's identity. We cannot find the self upon which we rest our pride.

The man with a truthful heart is best:
there is no happiness without the truth,
no matter how many millions of times
one tries to find it by other means.

TWS PP180

Any happiness not founded in reality is under constant threat. Ignorance involves an effort to avoid any facts that expose our flawed beliefs. With a love of truth, we need not spend our efforts to protect ourselves from facts. If one of our beliefs turns out to be false, then we are grateful to know. Kabir points to the desire to be intimate with the truth and share it with others. Whether we are in joy or pain, both of those are better when they arise from truth rather than falsehood. We might praise ourselves as honest by taking a vow of silence, but that is not the same thing as being truthful. Let us speak the truth as best we can and correct our mistakes as we go. If tyrants deprive us of our tongue, then we write, touch or glance at others with understanding. We share whatever truth we can slip past our physical limits. A question arises as to whether we can ever really speak the truth and Kabir acknowledges the limits of words in what follows.

If I say one, it isn't so.
If I say two, it's slander.
Kabir has thought about it.
As it is, so it is.

TBoK PP103

A truism can only be petty to one who already understands it. Almost two centuries before Berkley argued about the mind's involvement in all perceptions, Kabir speaks of the problem. He bypasses the question about the world existing inside or outside of the observer. Kabir is more concerned with the misery brought about by self-deception and the consequences of clinging to false beliefs when we find them preferable to facts. The ideas about the things we explain will taint our words and corrupt honesty. We, like the poet, can only do our best within our limits. Most of us have been shocked to find something we believed and repeated to be false. If our error remained undiscovered, then we would have continued repeating something bogus. The willingness to be wrong remains the only way to be devoted to the truth. We cannot steal the truth from the words about it anymore than the word candy tastes sweet.

> **Who are you, and whence do you**
> **come?**
> **Where dwells that supreme spirit, and**
> **how does He have His sport with**
> **all created things?**
> **The fire is in the wood; but who**
> **awakens it suddenly? Then it**
> **turns to ashes, and where goes the**
> **force of the fire?**
> **The true guru teaches that He has**
> **neither limit nor infinitude.**
> **Kabir says: "Brahma suits his language**
> **to the understanding of His**
> **hearer."**

SoK PP92

Anyone who tries to describe an experience knows that the description is not the same as the feeling or event. The grey areas of language invite inaccuracy and deceit. We use words loosely and habitually, but we can also speak consciously. The poet boldly seeks a greater understanding on the part of the listener and admits the limits of the words he chooses to speak.

No one knows the secret of the weaver
who spread his warp through the universe.
He dug two ditches, sky and earth,
made to spools, sun and moon,
filled his shuttle with a thousand threads,
and weaves till today: a difficult length!
Kabir says, they're joined by actions.
Good threads and bad,
that fellow weaves both.

TBoK PP84

Nobody knows how existence came to be. Science provides the best current guess that withstands scrutiny until a better one comes along. Now, consider the pretenders who presume to know about the creation of the universe. Some people who believed in superstitious ideas probably became our teachers when we were young. We must dare to see beyond our learned prejudices, or we are likely to miss good things. People have often held dogmatically to falsehoods in the hopes of a better world. Just consider the ideologies that have sought to create some kind of perfect society by purging the world of the unorthodox. The various attempts to create a utopia throughout history have left many rotting corpses in their wake. Human belief in any utopian ideal has never led to any perfection, despite the millions killed. We should have learned our lesson by now. Our religious wars, Bolshevism, and fascism seem to be a collective version of a mistake often made by individuals in their personal lives. We want good things and wish to avoid bad things. However, to imagine a supreme state and then by comparison, reject good things because they are inferior to an abstract idea is a mistake. Stated differently, good and bad are interwoven. On our own, we can turn our world into hell by trying to make it a heaven. Consider a lover imagining a world of bliss if only the other would play his or her part properly. Such an idealistic lover can blame any other who is unable or unwilling to live within the confines of a concept. The idealistic partner may feel robbed of the joy promised by the belief and become coercive in an attempt to control those they love. The idealistic partner sacrifices good things outside of the ideal because they seem inferior next to the excellence in his or her mind. The mistake of the idealist is like rejecting a fruit that has a bruise for an imagined fruit that can never abate hunger. There are unforeseen events in life that bring forth good things that don't conform to our narrow-mindedness.

> **Gorakh was yoga's connoisseur.**
> **They didn't cremate**
> **his body.**
> **Still his meat rotted and mixed**
> **with dust. For nothing**
> **he polished his body.**

TBoK PP94

Beware sacrificing what we can have for an impossible or even a highly doubtful ideal. To believe in an afterlife or continuous rebirth is not only conceptual, but is also an attempt to achieve perfection through something perishable. Not only do we have reason to doubt such wishful thinking, but those who pretend to have such knowledge manipulate large groups of people and have sent many to their graves seeking eternal bliss.

> **Moving within limits: Man.**
> **Moving without limits: Saint.**
> **Dropping both limits and no-limits-**
> **unfathomable thought.**

TBoK PP112

Let us do the inconceivable as our poet suggests and drop the ideas of both man and saint. We need to let go of the burden of both and see with eyes unburdened by colored lenses.

> **Kabir's house is at the top**

> of a narrow, slippery track.
> An ant's foot won't fit.
> So, villain,
> why load your bullock.

TBoK PP93

This weaver lived poor, indeed there are few who would aspire to his fortunes. To partake of his rich generosity, we must step outside of the mind for a few moments and arrest our thinking and fantasy. Will we dare to walk this path when what we believe ourselves to be cannot possibly make the journey?

> Why so impatient, my heart?
> He watches over the birds,
> beasts, and insects,
> He who cared for you whilst you were
> yet in your mother's womb,
> Shall He not care for you now that you are come forth?
> Oh my heart, how could you turn from
> the smile of your Lord and wonder
> so far from him?
> You have left your Beloved and are
> thinking of others: and this is
> why all your work is in vain.

SoK PP106

I fault the above poem or, at least, the translation which talks of the unarticulated life that abides regardless of our concepts about it. With the word *He,* the above verse gives a false human shape to the complete creative process of life itself, from the simplest vegetation to the human. Elsewhere, Kabir calls this unfolding of life *the nameless one*; this un-title is better at indicating what embraces both form and formlessness. This unnamable one is life that grew in your mother's womb. The word *He,* historically carries with it the impression of a deity. Kabir attempts here to describe the life that abides in us before our ego usurped our attention. This life embodies the consciousness where ideas of self rise and fall. This consciousness is also a refuge from our fabricated fears concerning any imagined ego. We can imagine souls and gods, endowing them with various traits and constructing any nonsense necessary according to these ideas. Once we identify ourselves with the products of our mind, we judge ourselves. We compare our *beliefs about ourselves* against *our beliefs about others,* who ironically, may be doing the same, while we all stand in a queue waiting for our impending death.

> **I have stilled my restless mind, and**
> **my heart is radiant: for in That-**
> **Ness I have seen beyond That-Ness,**
> **in company I have seen the comrade himself.**
> **Living in bondage, I have set myself**
> **free: I have broken away from**
> **the clutch of all narrowness.**
> **Kabir says: "I have attained the**
> **unattainable, and my heart is**
> **colored with the color of love."**

SoK PP95

Our ideas of self are a ghost called ego, it takes up residence in our mind and haunts us. In order to maintain a vision of self as something more than thought we avoid many facts (e.g., the moment we do not think about ourselves, our so-called self disappears and we still exist). Our sense of self is unsustainable, regardless of being an entrenched habit. We learn to govern our choices by pursuing experiences or circumstances valuable to this supposed self. What we usually mean by the word freedom is an ability to choose. Choice, like the word freedom, is vague and abstract. Our ability to choose should not be limited to a definition, such as the ability to pursue what we desire. An ass may pull a cart in pursuit of a desired carrot that a master dangles in front of its face. The master can yield the carrot to the beast when the work is over. I hope we agree that this enslaved animal *choosing* to pursue a desire is not what we mean when we discuss our ability to choose. Remember, the carrot is at least a thing that the donkey can actually eat. Many undeserving authorities appeal to our desires by offering immaterial objects of thought, mere concepts dangled in front of us so we will pull another kind of cart. In this case, what motivates our actions need never be realized to maintain its power to motivate us. That actuating force is our own power to conceive of future benefits, in this life or another.

We can remain ignorant of our awareness by taking it for granted in experience and by fixating on the passing experiences. People say they fell into dreamless sleep and experienced nothing for hours but neglect the awareness that reports that nothing passed across the screen of the mind. What is that consciousness? This neglect of awareness is being in the clutch of the narrowness that Kabir mentions above.

The only thing unattainable and, at the same time, possessed is awareness because we assume awareness in any experience. We can't grasp awareness as an object because the minute we think about awareness the concept we create becomes an object of thought in awareness and we move in circles. We are limited to the physical and mental capacity of our organism itself, but do not confuse this limit of our physical abilities with the restraints of narrow-mindedness or prejudice.

If we believe our ideas of self are what constitutes who we are, then we are imposing arbitrary limits. Kabir opens a door to life and love beyond a demand for particular outcomes. Kabir has more choices because he is not identifying himself with any outcome. In the above poem, the poet gives away a secret, stilling the turbulent mind.

A woman I know suspected her doctor of exaggerating her blood pressure. She tested herself in different drugstores as time went on. All of the results confirmed the physician's conclusion. She thought the different machines either must be broken or were fraudulent. Then, she awoke blind in one eye. The stroke exposed her error. Every illusion we create has a shadow of disillusionment stalking it.

We can habitually conceive the reality around us. A great deal of what we call significance, we create in our minds. We submerge ourselves in judgments of the world based on existing notions. Then, something unexpected happens. When we feel our egos threatened, our emotions run high, inundating us with all manner of concerns, some relevant and some fantasy. Our abstraction of the world must be much smaller and far less detailed than the world in which we live. When we live consciously, our doubts open us to see more than our habits of mind will allow.

> **The mind: a mad killer-elephant.**
> **The mind's desires: hawks.**
> **They can't be stopped by chants or charts.**
> **When they like, they swoop and eat.**
>
> TBoK PP106

We mistake our habits for who we are. Sometimes, we discover a strong inclination poorly adapted to the real world. The fact that the habit reasserts itself can be shocking or irksome, but it does not justify itself. Do not mistake the strength of a habit as proof of anything. Many times, people feel something must be wrong with them and even seek a pathological explanation because a bad tendency returns. The secret is that we cannot relegate the act of breaking habits into a habit itself.

Consider trying the following experiment. If we consciously watch the activity of our thinking for two hours, we might strip the mind of some credibility. If we asserted all our thoughts, then we would probably look crazy. Many people try to control their minds by focusing on something that they can do, like work. Others rely on various diversions as an alternative to being alone with the lunatics in their skulls. Our needs for avoidance often lead to using others to escape from our own mental torments. Under this duress of needing reassurance, we confirm the ideas of our coworkers, friends, and lovers if they will pretend the same for us.

Kabir impugns the mind as a conman that we cannot live without. To do anything, we must use the mind as a tool, but that does not mean that we live in a tool shed. We can add more tools and remove the obsolete or broken ones. Once we understand that our mind imposes beliefs and ideas upon ourselves and the world, no God or religion can be our master and we can replace any idea with one better suited to the facts. We realize that facts may change tomorrow, allowing us to reform our ideas. Once we recognize that we are dealing with a trickster, we can be careful not to become a dupe.

We live in a world of temporary explanations that we try to improve as we grasp more reality. For example, a man sees the outline of a woman in the distance, his interest is provoked and he wants to catch a glimpse of her face. Then, he realizes that the person that he saw was a man! Oops. The narrative changes according to the person's reality unless he has the good fortune to have the same interest in both sexes. The interpretation of facts goes on constantly and the same process of testing our deductions with trial and error becomes methodical in science. Kabir has a suggestion as an alternative to being frustrated with the trials and setbacks of discovery: accept this entire wonderful life adventure and love it! Somehow, we've got into this circus tent of life; let us enjoy the show. Unfortunately, we may not understand and will make ourselves miserable.

Woe be unto the man or woman who identifies themselves with any experience or person because those things are bound to change. If having a beautiful wife is a sign that one is good, then it must signify something too when her beauty fades or she gives her love to someone else. Simply take the previous sentence above and exchange the word wife for money, power, property, prestige or anything one can attain and then revisit the content. This exercise illuminates things that we mistakenly take to be proof of who we are.

Monkey and organ-grinder,
creature and mind.
He makes it leap and dance,
he leads it off by the hand.

TBoK PP100

It does not seem so long ago that we were much younger. What have we been doing since? Do we chase the next desire or diversion, while the moments of our lives pass by our eyes as if they were endless? Our minds repeatedly crank out desires. If we could have attained security or fulfillment through our satisfactions, would we not have accomplished these things by now? If these satisfactions are only temporary, then our identification with having or not having these things must be misguided.

When our dream is love, we feel passions like sexual desire. When our dreams become nightmares, the fear engulfs us. We may forget the same mind that dreams at night is active while awake in a different way. While awake, our consciousness includes the sensations of the world *and* the affective power of our mind to induce feelings just as in dreams. We can experience the same intensity of emotion anytime as we do while dreaming, but, when awake, we would be wise to discern between publicly observable facts, and the interpretations, distortions and falsehoods that can be found only in our minds. Such clarity is less common than we might think. We jump like frogs flicking their tongues at flies on a video; the poor creatures mistake the screen of an iPad for their dinner. We spend much time struggling with reflections in our minds. These cerebral enchantments lay hidden in our habits of thinking.

Mind-ocean, mind-born waves -
many unconscious ones drown.
Kabir says, he is saved
whose heart can discern.

TBoK PP101

Our narrow ideas of the world based on a conjured self need not be a tyrannical force in our lives. Kabir wants to give us an option other than endless seeking. He is not simply saying that you should do such and such and you will attain this and that. We cannot attain our self because we cannot be other than what we truly are. He directs us to the self that cannot be lost as we witness the mental idea of self rise and fall like waves on water.

> **The mind, greedy for its own juice,**
> **splashes in sensual waves.**
> **Mind drives, body rides-**
> **thus everything runs away.**

TBoK PP118

We can shock ourselves with feelings and can turn our days into a stage for tragedy. Sometimes, our ideals of the way things should be give rise to contempt of the ordinary. Routinely, we hide behind words like *preference*, treating events outside our beliefs as unwelcome or dangerous. Pointing to our history, we justify what we want and rely on prejudice to enforce restrictions. We fear that we will lose imagined future opportunities and this dread causes us to doubt the many good things that we could have.

What yearning should we indulge in order to gain contentment when all of our senses seek satisfaction? Many wishes can only be satisfied briefly and others not at all. We say that some desires are better than the others, so we ornament them with regalia and honor. In America, we learn to admire success even if what someone does to succeed is reprehensible. We learn what desires to respect but many of our teachers may have been prejudiced even if they were well meaning. Having the ability to suppress a desire to kill someone can be an extremely good thing. I have seen parents suppress artistic desire in a child for fear the child won't make a good living. If this child matures and becomes rich selling insurance that cheats customers, the parents will probably believe they did a good job. Such a salesman is an example of what happens when what is second rate gets first preference. Humanity is rank with mistaken value judgments.

**In a moment, apocalypse-
heads whirl.
Afraid of the future,
they howl at the past.**

TBoK PP121

We conjure our tomorrows as if the future is bound to our concepts. We may say "no person knows everything," but, still, we coddle our hubris by measuring all things by what we know. This arrogance is why entirely new things can seem familiar. By ignoring facts and reasons contrary to our beliefs, we invite life experiences to rip faulty beliefs from our terrified grasp when we could have let those beliefs go, just as we do with dreams in the morning.

"If you do not expect the unexpected, you will not find it; for it is hard to be sought out..."

Heraclitus

Presuming to know is different from trial and error. Generalizing is not bad, but we tend to treat our schemes as facts. In any group of people, unfounded beliefs pose great peril when the popularity of an idea takes the place of proof. For example, the delusional thinking of Americans imagining an imminent threat brought about a preemptive war and a river of bloodshed.

"We don't want the smoking gun to be a mushroom cloud."[vii]

Condoleezza Rice

Rice was afraid of a conceived future and perhaps she did not know that the peril she took action to avoid was imaginary. The reason for war ceased to be convincing when discovery proved no significant threat. The repetition of apocalyptic rhetoric led to disasters and the ideas of how to manage the aftermath proved even worse.

Throw out unworthy thoughts,

make the best of your birth.
Give up the gait of a
Crow, come to me like a swan.

TBoK PP119

We may be tempted to view the pursuit of truth as a way to achieve the results that we hold in our minds. The problem with viewing veracity only as means instead of part of a whole is that it suggests that what we desire has the value separate from anything true. Without understanding the loss, we may abandon the truth to pursue what we think precious. If we seduce a lover with lies, we abase the merit of the situation as a whole. Moreover, an exposé of the truth becomes a threat. When we achieve ends without integrity, we lose something extremely valuable. For example, let us imagine two men, Mr. West and Mr. East, who both love a third, whom we will call Mr. North, who is an unscrupulous rogue. Mr. West imagines Mr. North to be decent and harmless and has the satisfaction of having a splendid friend in him. Mr. West inadvertently misleads others by misrepresenting the rascal as benign. Mr. East also enjoys his love of Mr. North, but disapproves of and criticizes his many faults. I suggest that Mr. East is more fortunate then Mr. West. Moreover, Mr. East's love has greater value because it is rooted in the truth, not only for him, but for others as well. The truth does not threaten Mr. East. Anyone who agrees with this judgment admits that truth and love form a whole with greater value then love without truth.

If we think that the truth will shelter and protect us, then what we want is security. The misery we create trying to make the world safe for our ego disappears when we cease to demand that end. We stop believing that the failure to accomplish some desire suggests that we are personally flawed. Consider how some lovers feel that they will die without the other lover, a dangerous belief indeed. With or without such artificial thinking, we can put on our warm socks and meet our beloved in the park. If this lover says goodbye forever, we still exist with our wonderful socks. We need not grasp at vapors in the mind and cling to beliefs that tell us who we are due to our involvement in a relationship. We can avoid the misery that results from identification with circumstances, but, to do that, we must clear the cobwebs from our minds, even if they happen to be cherished beliefs.

A raft of tied-together snakes
in the world-ocean.
Let go, and you'll drown.
Grasp, and they'll bite your arm.

TBoK PP103

Let us differentiate the inestimable benefits of accumulated knowledge from the tendency to hold fast to the past out of fear of the unknown. The beliefs we cling to, particularly about ourselves, are a denial of the growth of knowledge. When our habits have a stronger impact on us than facts, we are in danger of rejecting discovery in return for a mental storyline about the world and ourselves. For thousands of years, it was the belief that man cannot fly; however, innovation exposed this belief as false. No reason exists to think that a new understanding could not grant us many choices beyond our current beliefs about the world and ourselves.

The mind is a nervous thief,
the mind is a pure cheat.
The ruin of sages, men and gods,
the mind has a hundred thousand gates.

TBoK PP100

Consider the way we can chew gum automatically and forget that we are doing it. We can use the mind fully aware that we are doing so, but we can also easily let it run on autopilot. We often swap one habit for another, like putting in a new piece of gum. Many flavors exist, but, eventually, the gum becomes flavorless. Thinking about ourselves may be one of our oldest habits and not following in this rut will take a conscious choice.

The longing to be free of habit is born of recognizing unnecessary limits. The unconscious mind is a citadel of habit and we must intentionally leave the confines of its walls. When we do, we can strip our tendency for habit of its ruling power and relegate it to the menial tasks to which it is best suited.

Delusion filled three worlds,
delusion everywhere.
Kabir says (and he's thought about it),
you live in Delusion Village.

TBoK PP120

If we treat knowledge as hypothetical, then we lose nothing but a false sense of certainty. Let us not pretend emphatic self-assurance to be a guarantee of anything; after all, many great fools have confidence. Consider one woman who filched valuables from a deceased relative's house. She feared unscrupulous family members would steal these things if she did not take them for safekeeping. With this power of rationalizing, anything can mean something else. A falsehood sometimes gives us a much stronger emotional impression than the facts. We may be alone, but if we believe an intruder is in the house with us, the fact that the idea is untrue makes little difference to the feeling experience.

Nearby they sink and don't come up;
it makes me wonder.
In illusions swift stream,
how can you slumber?

TBoK PP97

People learn to see themselves in terms of their current state of affairs. When things are difficult, it can seem hard to devote attention to breaking bad habits. Then again, what reason is there to surrender any belief or tendency when all is well? In this way, both good times and hard times tend toward inertia. I have seen people convinced that they discovered a law of abundance after a few months of good fortune.

A friend of mine related a profound story about a colleague that I repeat. During the economic boom early in the 21st century, one life coach had a business teaching that monetary reward would follow spiritual understanding. People possessing wealth found this idea most agreeable. Those credulous individuals with less pleasant circumstances looked upon the fortunate as proof of the abundance belief. The teacher probably believed it himself. When the bubble burst, his clients, along with their money, disappeared and the life coach wanted to die. This leader of others apparently faced the horrifying prospect of getting a real job. Moreover, the turn of fortune exposed his beliefs to the purifying fire of change.

We assume our expectations are correct when indulging any habit. When dealing with variable things, such as other people, we practically beg for misery when we respond habitually. When we act according to habits, we treat habits as facts until we see unwanted results. When people grumble that it is hard to consciously abandon habits, I point to any obvious connection between their miseries and their habits and then ask if that pain is easy. This statement usually makes the point.

Like drunks driving a car, many of us only learn the hard way. As long as we seem to be getting away with foolishness, we will do it again. When we live on autopilot, our biases gain momentum; they rule our actions and impose limits that we take for granted. Most of us have said to a friend at some point, "Why are you saying that (emotionally charged thing) to me? You should be saying that to the relevant person." The reply is typically something like, "I could never say that to him or her!" Obviously, such a man or woman just said whatever it was and could repeat it to another person. Such a declared inability seems bewildering when the subject seems trivial. These decrees, with few exceptions, are as false as they are common.

Make the guru your burnisher,
polish, polish your mind.
Scour with the word.

Make consciousness a mirror.

TBoK PP107

We use a reflection in the mirror, but we do not mistake the image for anything other than a representation. Keep the mirror clean and the reflection will be more precise. Nevertheless, remember, our likeness is not alive. If we forget, we will feel threatened by anything that affects the image, even when it does not threaten what the mirror echoes in likeness.

Entered in the body,
sitting there aware.
What state do you want?
Thus insight is given.

TBoK PP128

A habitual cynic feels precisely what any negative person would, it is a self-fulfilling prophesy. We add meaning to the conditions around us and, in doing so, change our understanding of the circumstances. For example, an Islamist's mind adds a negative impression to seeing an unveiled Muslim woman in public. The Islamist interprets the facts through a belief. The same kind of thinking often happens when considering a woman's beauty. We arrogantly believe our mental representations to be the way the world actually is; if we find the world flawed, we must also be imagining how it should be instead. We compare our questionable beliefs of the world to a fictional better world and find the world as we see it lacking by contrast.

I have been thinking of the difference
between water and the waves on it. Rising,
water's still water, falling back,
it is water, will you give me a hint
how to tell them apart?
Because someone has made up the word
"wave," do I have to distinguish it from water?
There is a Secret One inside us;

> **the planets in all the galaxies**
> **pass through his hands like beads.**
> **That is a string of beads one should look at with**
> **luminous eyes.**
>
> TKB PP29

Our experiences are the beads Kabir refers to in the above poem. These experiences include all the truths, misrepresentations and falsehoods that we know. In our awareness, a sense of self arises like a wave on the sea of consciousness. If we do not identify ourselves with the ego rising and falling in the mind, then we will not add useless strife to the ebb and flow. We vulnerably experience the newness of the ocean and it is sometimes a lot of fun, but we should not underestimate the waves lest they sweep us out to sea. The thread of a human life has many surprising events and few things liberate our capabilities like recognition of the unpredictable environment around us.

> **The Holy One disguised as an old person**
> **in a cheap hotel**
> **goes out to ask for carfare.**
> **But I never seem to catch sight of him.**
> **If I did, what would I ask him for?**
> **He has already experienced what is missing in my**
> **life.**
> **Kabir says: I belong to this old person.**
> **Now let the events about to come, come!**
>
> TKB PP51

Somehow, matter has become conscious in human form, this living consciousness is the holy one and it is in all of us. Before we rot, we should know that life is something other than what we think. This point would be trivial if people acknowledged it, but many do not. Those individuals who pretend to be who they think they are must struggle with events that push them beyond their expectations, even when those unforeseen events are beautiful. Not only is the poet aware of his limits and lack of control, but he also knows what he must eventually lose. It is because of this lack of pretense that he can stand boldly as a part of life, not apart from life.

> **There is a flag no one sees blowing in the**
> **sky Temple.**
> **A blue cloth has been stretched up,**
> **it is decorated with the moon and many jewels.**
> **The sun and the moon can be seen in that place;**
> **when looking at that, bring your mind down to**
> **silence.**
> **I will tell you the truth:**
> **the man who has drunk from that liquid wanders**
> **around like someone insane.**

TKB PP14

On a clear evening, you have probably gazed upon the stars and, for a moment, lost yourself. If you have the luck to possess eyes, then you should not miss the celestial splendor. Looking at the stars costs nothing and the greatest thief cannot steal them from you. People value gems, but, when we gaze at jewels, they are imposters reflecting light from another source. Everyone holds the celestial treasures in common and, thus, they have little or no value as means. When we feel staggered by astronomical beauty, we forget ourselves and the doors of the temple beyond superstition open to us. We see the light, but may take little note of the background. I do not only mean the darkness between the radiant points in the sky, but, also, our own awareness that our sensations of the stars and beauty come and go within. Consciousness is that space between two thoughts that is in the background when thoughts and sensation have our attention. This consciousness also abides when we are absorbed in habits. In a similar way, our sensations and thoughts exist in a consciousness that we probably take for granted. To notice this consciousness is meditation.

Let us inquire into the self that abides in life before, during and after any of our temporary experiences. We do not see consciousness and it is not a sight itself or a concept about who we are. Awareness stands in the midst of feeling, before and after the sensation has passed. We cannot oblige this awareness to fulfill our wishes, but we can avoid the mistake of trying to prove who we are by adding arbitrary meaning to our experiences.

Scrutinizing Religion

It's a heavy confusion.
The Veda, Koran, holiness, hell, woman, man,
a clay pot shot with air and sperm...
When the pot falls apart, what do you call it?
Numbskull! You've missed the point.
It's all one skin and bone, one piss and shit,
one blood, one meat.
From one drop, a universe.
Who's Brahman? Who's Shudra?
Brahma rajas, Shiva tamas, Vishnu sattva...
Kabir says, plunge into Ram!
There: No Hindu. No Turk.

TBoK PP67

Once we brand something, we are tempted to forget that the name is arbitrary. Nothing comes identified. This poem appeals to discernment and has a bitter taste. Kabir pleads for us to distinguish what has value and not lose ourselves in words. He holds the mirror of reality up to authority and gives us a choice to make the jump from ideas to life.

Christians, Hindus and Muslims, blacks and whites, higher and lower castes, and classes are categories that lump people together like crated produce. When we accept these brands, we cannot help, but admire those individuals who are *better* according to those beliefs. This admiration makes us imitators. Throughout history, human deference (or groveling) to people in power made heroes and saints out of the butchers of mankind. Hiding behind status, pomp and ritual, charlatans manufacture and offer a false sense of both importance and security. Regardless of any title, we all still shit and die. We also hold in common the ability to deceive ourselves.

The great went off in their greatness,
ego and every hair.

71

Without knowing the guru all
four casts are untouchable.

TBoK PP105

We fear letting go of superstitions and biased beliefs that pretend to explain the world and ourselves. Many who imagined a limit on what females could accomplish have been as wrong as those individuals who said that humans would never fly. For centuries, women appeared inferior, not just to men, but to women as well. People viewed (many still do) women through the distorting lens of sexual bias. If the example of women contradicting so many beliefs of sexism will not convince you that the explanations that we take for truths are doubtful, then I wonder what will. Sometimes it is wonderful to be wrong!

From holy man you turned to thief,
from thief to social worker.
You'll never know what life is
till the blows come down on you.

TBoK PP107

Anyone lost in a narrative about who they themselves are, must retreat from the facts that expose bogus notions. Life can be a fierce master delivering shocks that will shatter the ego. A sophisticated idealist hides his malevolence, not only from others, but also from himself as he is convinced that he is a *good person*. He will have no mercy because good people have no need of mercy. We may think it unfair that ordinary people following authority also endure any misguided consequences of that deference. Pretenders manipulate the average person by using the fictional ghost as a weapon. We make terrible mistakes believing in the ghost of our identity. Now consider kind people who give generously often play the sophist when they defend an identity. I am not talking here about intentional hypocrites like many cunning politicians. I am talking about people who do a fair day's work and go out of their way to help others.

"There is only one way to hide being unloving from yourself and others, and that is to give the appearance of being a loving person." [viii]

Todd Vickers

The specter of self haunts those of us who do not understand it as a mental object.

The fish in the water
is racked by thirst:
I hear about it
and burst out laughing.
What you're looking for
is right at home:
and yet you roam from forest to forest,
full of gloom.
Without self-knowledge
the world is all make-believe:
what's Mathura
what's Kashi?

TWS PP200

Kashi, also known as Varanasi, is one of India's holiest cities along the banks of the Ganges. Believers say that dying in this place automatically brings salvation. Kabir lived his life in this city. When he prepared for death, he traveled to Mathura, a city of spiritual abhorrence. He made his death a challenge against the prejudices of those individuals who loved him. The end of his life became an invitation out of the trap of narrow-mindedness. His actions showed that he could disobey the popular belief. He used his own death as a message of love, as a way for others to find their way out of superstition.

Tell me, O pandit,
what place is pure-

where can I sit
and eat my meal?
Mother was impure,
father was impure—
the fruit they bore
were also impure.
They arrived impure,
they left impure—
unlucky folks,
they died impure.
My tongue's impure,
my words are impure,
my ears, my eyes,
they're all impure—
you Brahmans,
you've stolen the fire,
but you can't burn off
the impurity of the senses!
The fire, too, is impure,
the water's impure—
so even the kitchen's
nothing but impure.
The ladle's impure
that serves a meal,
and they're impure
who sit and eat their fill.
Cowdung's impure,
the bathing-square's impure—
it's very curbs
are nothing but impure.
Kabir says,
only they are pure

**who've completely cleansed
their thinking.**

TWS PP124

Consider this metaphor for someone trapped in the mind seeking escape. Once, I saw a beautiful moth crawling along one of the many windowpanes in a hospital. It beat its wings against the glass. It sensed the sunlit world beyond the transparent obstacle, but it remained trapped inside. The creature explored the different windows seeking release. I tried to help, but its delicate body made catching it impossible. A life and death event unfolded as I tried to guide the moth to an opening with my hands. Sadly, this lovely living thing flew to a window beyond my reach and I left it to its fate. Turning back, I saw its beautiful wings battering another pane, still searching. I pondered the little carcasses that adorned the windowsills nearby. Soon after, I saw an insect buzzing around my house. I opened the door and waved my hands wildly. He flew out the opening and I never saw him again. Kabir's lyrics gesture emphatically to liberate us from a trap fashioned of the beliefs through which we view the world.

Having our fictional ideas of self destroyed by facts usually causes despair. Arresting our habits, through disillusionment, can be excruciating. After the collapse of identity, we may construct a new identity or try to patch up the old ego. This destruction and creation of identity can happen many times. The ego is the only thing we have reason to believe capable of reincarnation. We can easily miss the chance to make better choices, while we struggle to recreate or maintain any ideas of self.

**Pandit, look in your heart for knowledge.
Tell me where untouchability
came from, since you believe in it.
Mix red juice, white juice and air-
a body bakes in a body.
As soon as the eight lotuses**

are ready, it comes
into the world. Then what's
untouchable?
Eighty-four hundred thousand vessels
decay into dust, while the potter
keeps slapping clay
on the wheel, and with a touch
cuts each one off.
We eat by touching, we wash
by touching, from a touch
the world was born.
So who's untouched? Asks Kabir.
Only she
who's free from delusion.

TBoK PP55

Anyone with a mind can be deluded; they can take thought to be more than thought. When we suffer, we look to solve that problem. Quieting our mind may seem impossible if we are miserable but if our mind is creating the problem, the misery will continue until that manufacturing process stops. People use various means to arrest their mind, but the means used to get relief from our mind can themselves become a destructive habit. Drugs are an obvious example but we do other things that are not as blatant as drug use. Ritual and spiritual practice can alter our states and become unconscious and redundant. People identify themselves with their spirituality. A spiritual ego leads straight back into delusion because now you have another identity to create, sustain and defend. Kabir suggests throwing out religion and going directly into silent self inquiry.

Doubting what takes place only in thought will not cost us anything. Quietness of the mind reveals that we are not obliged to any mental object. Thought is harmless until we believe it and, then, superstitions become invisible tyrants, imposing themselves upon us.

> **Teaching and preaching, their mouths**
> **filled up with sand.**
> **While they watched the fields of others,**
> **their own crops were eaten.**

TBoK PP126

Compare the prejudices of our own time with those prejudices of the past. The musty ancient gods also had their respected representatives. The Greek oracles were indicative of these types throughout history, the ignorant authorities presumed to direct the courses of people's lives. The creators of these persuasive fictions are now as dead as the credulous they misled. The temptation to grant authority remains extremely great today. Someone wears robes and herds of ordinary people grant deference to that person. For the price of repeating words from a book, one appears wise to the credulous. Misery germinates when we yield to those individuals who use deceptive power, be they demagogues, groups or lovers. The current evidence used to support religion rests on grounds just as shaky as the deities worshiped in the past whose names we've never heard. Do not be fooled by a façade appealing to a dream. Those in the past who persuaded men that Odin road on an eight legged horse also made men willing to die in battle. Many people today are just as willing to kill and die for similar reasons.

> **Who speak sweet words from the mouth**
> **and keep something else in the heart-**
> **Kabir says, Ram is even cleverer**
> **than those people.**

TBoK PP120

Death remains the great equalizer of people. Nothing, not even the great sun in the sky, can stand against change. It is a strange juxtaposition that ideas can be more fragile than *our lives* because we can live on as new facts and understandings destroy our old beliefs. Still, many beliefs continue to influence people after their creators are long dead. There are ideas that go unquestioned and many beliefs govern people's lives regardless of being good, bad or false.

Seeing the mill turn
brings tears to the eyes.
No one who falls between the stones
comes out unbroken.

TBoK PP104

The religious are not the only ones who bind themselves to unfounded beliefs that can have horrible results. Professional people subject themselves to a fallacy similar to one that has haunted many musicians. Players esteeming the genius of Charlie Parker explained his creative powers by pointing out his use of heroin. They used the drug as a means to greatness and many musicians died like Parker, except many of them died without gaining the achievement desired. People successful in business can display destructive character traits and admirers attribute the successes to these dispositions. A deceitful and selfish man may have inside knowledge of the movement of a stock and may reap tremendous rewards as a result. Admirers may idolize and ape the cunning business man, his deceitfulness and selfishness, but may not have the same inside knowledge or success. Professional people make the same stupid mistake as the unfortunate musicians. These imitators do not ask how many people failed doing this same thing. Such a question can reveal the circumstantial reality of any particular success that can't be duplicated by playing monkey see, monkey do.

Kabir scolds groundless beliefs because the word candy gives no sweetness to the tongue and a parrot can speak the word truth without understanding the meaning. Facts are sacred things. Anyone who thinks that beliefs have more power than facts should consider how many of the former crumbled in front of the latter. We find the power to bring down gods and frauds in having a better understanding of facts.

We cannot live in a fictitious tower of objectivity. Real observation means being involved in what we understand. We witness the limits of our faculties, not only in our observations of the world, but in the inconsistencies between the evidence and what passes for wisdom.

> **There is nothing but water at the**
> **holy bathing places; and I know**
> **that they are useless, for I have**
> **bathed in them.**
> **The images [gods] are all lifeless, they cannot**
> **speak; I know, for I have cried**
> **aloud to them.**
> **The Purana and the Koran are mere**
> **words; lifting up the curtain, I**
> **have seen.**
> **Kabîr gives utterance to the words of**
> **experience; and he knows very**
> **well that all other things are un-**
> **true.**

SoK PP90

Many people would call the above verse intolerant, but Kabir neither persecutes nor limits anyone's choices. Do not confuse criticism with oppression. To challenge a belief by demonstrating a reason to think it false shows concern for others. Controversy is a difficult matter when one is in an extreme minority. Kabir expended the effort to help others in spite of the fact that the exertion did not raise him financially. His prose invites observation in judging beliefs.

We can misunderstand facts, but, if we wish to challenge our ideas beyond verbal scrutiny, then experience will show us what is untrue through trial and error. We have a sacred tool called experimentation and this long dead poet dares us to test our ideas. Furthermore, Kabir spoke this statement approximately three centuries before David Hume insisted experience was a formidable challenge to beliefs. Hume had the advantage of education; he learned the best scientific and logical methods of his time. Similar learning was not available to a poor weaver in 15th century India. Kabir grasped the understanding he used intuitively. To cultivate such reason, almost completely alone, and against the popular ideas of his day tells us a lot about the integrity and capacity of this poet.

> **What house can we call**
> **a house without fear?**
> **People succumb and pray**
> **to fear everywhere -**
> **so live fearlessly!**
> **The birth of light,**
> **the light of birth -**
> **they bare fruits and pearls**
> **made of glass.**
> **On the riverbank**
> **at the pilgrim- station,**
> **the mind doesn't find**
> **true belief -**
> **it remains entangled**
> **in ritual's, rights and wrongs.**
> **The measure of evil**
> **and the measure of good -**
> **the two are alike.**
> **The touchstone you need**
> **is in your house -**
> **give up your quest**
> **for other qualities.**
> **O Kabir,**
> **don't shed light**
> **on the name devoid of all qualities -**
> **let people know**

that object of knowledge
exactly as it is.

TWS PP107

Treat fear like an errand boy granted simple and specific tasks. Fear does not deserve a position of leadership. To say "live fearlessly" goes too far, for without fight or flight we lack something necessary as a response to danger. Still, when fear has excessive influence, the emotion inspires credulity that authority exploits. Beliefs can be good, bad or false based on how closely they resemble reality. Beliefs of any quality can explain away the dread of the unknown. Religions are guilty of propagating many shoddy beliefs. Little would remain of many scriptures without threats of punishment. Religion manufactures fear, which makes the promised reward seem more valuable in contrast. The secular world has its versions of devotion as well, including the pretensions of the cunning corporate foot licker who shows deference to his masters with expectations of rewards in return, women who insist that life will be better after cosmetic surgery and men who accumulate symbols of status for similar reasons.

Rama, pure Rama,
the Flawless One,
is different:
the Chaos scattered all around us
is tainted.
Creations contaminated,
the syllable OM
is sullied:
impurity has created
this unholy spread.
Brahma,
Shankara, Indra,
are smirched:
Govind with his gopis

is soiled.
Speech and sound
are foul,
the Vedas are stained:
impurity has perpetrated
so many forms.
Learning, reading, recitation,
the ancient books
are all corrupt:
knowledge, cheapened, mouthed for free,
is dirty.
The leaf in the oblation is rank,
the God in his shrine
is unclean:
infection serves
the infected.
Impurity dances,
impurity sings:
pollution displays
an infinite number
of guises.
The how and what, the when and where
of contamination:
it vanquishes
charity, goodness, austerity,
devotion.
Kabir says,
only one in a million
awakens to this:
but when he does,
he gives up what's tainted
and joins the incorruptible.

We can chase a make-believe future, but the reality will be different than the hope. Modern spirituality often peddles the consoling suggestion that one can alter facts with positive thought. Anyone who wonders about the power of positive thinking might try an experiment. Shit on a plate and then think it into a delicious biscuit. Does the contemplative effort change the fact? If so, enjoy the lunch. Many darker members of our family buy chemicals to lighten their skin, conceiving a benefit. Now contrast them to those individuals with lighter complexions who rent tanning booths. Both are quite willing to risk the chemicals and radiation. Avoid wasting time and vitality endowing trivial things with values that they do not possess.

Qazi, what book are you lecturing on?

Yak yak yak, day and night.

You never had an original thought.

Feeling your power, you circumcise-

I can't go along with that, brother.

If your God favored circumcision,

why didn't you come out cut?

If circumcision makes you a Muslim,

what do you call your women?

Since women are called man's other half,

you might as well be Hindus.

If putting on the thread makes you Brahman,

what does the wife put on?

That Shudra's touching your food, pandit!

How can you eat it?

Hindu, Muslim-where did they come from?

Who started this road?

Look hard in your heart, send out scouts:

where is heaven?

Now you get your way by force,

but when it's time for dying,
without Ram's refuge, says Kabir,
brother, you'll go out crying.

TBoK PP69

Our powers of conception come with a risk. Again, we use thought like paint on the canvas of our minds, using our fears and wants as the brushes. We create and judge not only the future, but, also, an image of our world today. Seekers often surrender this power of the mind to the direction of leaders. However, we no more live in our concepts than a painter can live in a world he fabricated. Some art, just like thought, will be a more realistic representation, but the images will always be different than the actual events. Such mind stuff becomes delusional when taken to be certain. Our predecessors spilled rivers of blood in deference to many beliefs that we now reject; however, it would be a mistake to think that the damage exists only in the extremes. Seducing the suggestible with ritual comes with a price when the aspirations for a better life are perverted or misguided.

O BROTHER! When I was forgetful,
my true guru showed me
the way.
Then I left off all rites and ceremonies,
I bathed no more in the holy
water:
Then I learned that it was I alone who
was mad, and the whole world
beside me was sane; and I had
disturbed these wise people.
From that time fourth I knew no more
how to roll in the dust in obeisance.
I do not ring the temple bell:
I do not set the idol on the throne:
I do not worship the image with flowers.

**It is not with the austerities that mortify the
flesh which are pleasing to the Lord,
When you leave off your clothes
and kill your senses, you do not please the Lord:
The man who is kind and practices
righteousness, who remains passive
amidst the affairs of the world,
who considers all creatures on
earth as his own self,
He attains the immortal being, the
true God is ever with him.
Kabir says: "He attains the true
name whose words are pure,
and who is free from pride and conceit."**

SoK PP108

The end of obeisance means the end of pretending that holy authority and scriptures have access to impenetrable secret knowledge. We should not mistake Kabir's absence of respect to mean that he thinks all knowledge is of equal value. Kabir refuses to submit to hollow superiors and this refusal made him appear obnoxious and even crazy to obedient people.

Kabir uses the language of his contemporaries - Lord, immortal being, true God - and then ends with the attainment of the true name, which suggests that the other names listed in the poem are not true. For the modern person, I suggest interpreting the word *passive* as *receptive*.

Kabir does not here refer to sight, the seen or any concept of the seer. He points to the receptive awareness that remains even if we lose our eyes and only unending darkness remains. Instead, he tells the reader to notice the being that still abides with or without religious ideas.

**This is the big fight, King Ram.
Let anyone settle it who can.**

It's Brahma bigger or where he came from?
Is the Veda bigger or where it was born from?
Is the mind bigger or what it believes in?
Is Ram bigger or the knower of Ram?
Kabir turns round, it's hard to see-
is the holy place bigger, or the devotee?

TBoK PP23

People who fear the unknown are eager for superstition taught by a big shot. Some even prefer the more unintelligible to the plausible. Kabir's poems untie the ropes that bind our reason the way that Alexander solved the problem of the Gordian knot, only without the use of a sword. By stating the obvious, he exposes our spiritual explanations as human creations.

It is almost impossible to understand or even inquire into the self if we are unaware that we are imagining who we are and imagining gods. Any religious person might read this poem, think that his God is the gold that Kabir refers to and miss the point. What must be present in order to experience any perception or thought? Conscious life, meaning a life not automated by habits of the mind, is the treasure that Kabir indicates and what we commonly take for granted.

When you are imagining who you are, the reality remains the same regardless of who you imagine and regardless of the countless *isms* by which you identify your self.

O Sadhu! Purify your body in
the simple way.
As the seed is within the banyan tree,
and within the seed are the flowers,
the fruits, and the shade:
So the germ is within the body, and
within that germ is the body again.
The fire, the air, the water, the earth,
and the aether; you cannot have

> these outside of Him.
> O Kazi, O Pundit, consider it well:
> what is there that is not in the
> soul?
> The water-filled pitcher is placed upon
> water, it has water within and
> without.
> *It should not be given a name*, lest it
> call forth the error of dualism.
> Kabir says: "listen to the word, *the*
> *truth, which is your essence.* He
> speaks the Word to Himself; and
> He Himself is the Creator."

SoK PP93

We create the names of both gods and ourselves. No label is correct. The moment you think of a God to worship, there is a concept of self in relation to that God. This ego is a part of worship. The idea of self creates a sense of individuality in the ocean of life like Kabir's submerged pitcher. We are a little like a grape on a vine called life; this life existed for countless millennia before we were formed. These metaphors are something created. Words carry with them the error of dualism because the word and what the word represents are not the same thing.

> Makeshift man,
> witless, weightless,
> a red flower
> without fragrance.

TBoK PP129

We are constantly consulting an imaginary friend called self. Just as children mistake ideas for facts, our belief can make ideas appear as something more than thought.

> The Yogi dyes his garments, instead

of dying his mind in the
colors of love:
He sits within the temple of the Lord,
leaving Brahma to worship a stone.
He pierces holes in his ears, he has a
great beard and matted locks, he
looks like a goat:
He goes forth into the wilderness, killing
all his desires, and turned him
self into an eunuch:
He shaves his head and dyes his garments;
he reads the Gita and becomes
a mighty talker.
Kabir says: "you're going to the
doors of death, bound hand and
foot!"

SoK PP109

Why encourage people to worship other things when they are themselves an incarnation of matter, the embodiment of awareness itself?

If we feign respect for dubious popular beliefs, then cowardice hides behind decorum. To fault religious rites seems insolent, but these rights are questionable. Even religious people should not fault Kabir for criticizing beliefs, unless his words do not square with factual reality. Kabir does the hard work for us. We cannot know how many religious hypocrites lived secret lives that were never exposed. However, many scandals have stained the reputations of religious authorities; some, like child molesting priests, falsely enjoyed the admiration of others for rejecting sensuality.

Some people become grand simply *because* a herd of people praises them, like reality TV stars. Suggestible people are in danger when the individuals they admire lack merit. Herds are fickle and easily bored and people that desire to influence the crowd become seductive or bombastic. Those people who seek influence with groups often rely on rhetorical fireworks and extreme language to capture the attention of the audience. Demagogues are like the producers of pornography who keep pushing the limits of reason with wild stunts to catch the notice of distracted people. Both political and religious spectators, like sports fans, often repeat what trivia they hear, to impress others with their knowledge. This hearsay is one of the tools of propaganda. The value of such parroted knowledge remains a separate question.

Let us not console ourselves by imagining that the worst of beliefs abides in the past. Even if we omit current religious conflict as political, the fate of women under the auspices of custom is one inescapable measure of social coercion and violence. Even today, extremists throw acid in the faces of girls who don't dress conservatively or girls who dare to want an education. In Africa, fools hiding behind tradition literally slice off a girl's capacity for sexual joy. In the West, it seems that neutralizing women's sexuality also happens, using sexual shame instead of a knife. The shaming can go so deep that some women feel guilty for wanting pleasure; other women have a great difficulty finding sexual joy. Similar shaming affects men in different ways; the guilty conflict over the impulse for sexual joy creates unneeded stress. If we ignore the correlation between sexual dysfunction and the moral shaming typically rooted in religion, we are being willfully ignorant. Do not forget the cruelty of depriving a child of sex education, factual history, science or any of the best knowledge currently available. The withholding of reliable knowledge still happens in America today. Invariably religious-minded people are involved with such censorship. If you want to make your own judgments, leave admiration for holy showmen behind. To be fair, religious moderates do not cause the harm that fanatics do, but the same arguments from scripture justify moderates and extremists in their beliefs.

Have you heard the music that no fingers

enter into?
Far inside the house
entangled music-
What is the sense of leaving your house?
Suppose you scrub your ethical skin until it shines,
but inside there is no music,
then what?
Mohammed's son pours over words, and points out
this and that,
but if his chest is not soaked dark with love,
then what?
The Yogi comes along in his famous orange.
But if inside he is colorless, then what?
Kabir says: every instant that the Sun is risen,
if I stand in the temple, or on a balcony,
in the hot fields, or in a walled garden,
my own Lord is making love with me.

TKB PP55

Kabir reminds us of the crucial part of experience, consciousness itself, which abides within us. What value would any song have without a witness that is conscious of the music? We may take unlabeled awareness for granted when the richness of experience seizes our attention. Consciousness remains an inescapable necessity that we assume when we register feeling or cognition. Do not forget about this requisite by getting lost in sensual events. A good feeling, if maintained, offers little if any value outside of the awareness of the feeling. The absence of consciousness would neuter any sensation. On the other hand, asceticism mistakes what we experience as an obstacle for real knowledge. The ascetic throws the baby out with the bath water by confusing desire with a habitual identification with the desire.

As soon as they speak,
you recognize the ploys of saint and thief:

> **the workings of the inner self**
> **surface through the channel of the mouth.**
>
> TWS PP186

The saint and thief often use deceit to gain advantage. It may be that some holy men wish to help others, but that intention does not alter the means used. Perhaps spiritual pretenders are worse than pickpockets. The difference is that we may be able to replace stolen valuables, but we forever lose the time devoted to delusions.

> **They searched and searched, searched some more-**
> **it just kept disappearing.**
> **After all that search, when they couldn't find it,**
> **they gave up and said, "Beyond."**
>
> TBoK PP130

If we have become a holy fool, admitting the folly will take courage and more if any harm to others resulted from our actions. We must bear the unflattering admission of gullibility. Many in this position will find another spiritual leader to believe in and continue to surrender their judgments. This situation also happens to lovers who realize that they are misled. If we reject one liar, then we can find another easily who will play to our dreams. Disillusionment takes rare daring.

> **Veda, Purana: a blind man's mirror.**
> **Does the ladle taste the great flavor?**
> **Like a donkey loaded with sandalwood,**
> **a fool can't tell when the smell is good.**
> **Kabir says, they search the sky**
> **but don't find out**
> **how to quell their pride.**
>
> TBoK PP84

How do we expose both living and dead saints? We can ask what content remains in their words after disregarding everything imaginary (e.g., everything concerning the future). After the above discrimination, do the remaining public facts reconcile with their words? The future is necessarily imaginary and, when we visualize a heaven, hell or future life, we invent what these things mean about ourselves.

"The perfume of spiritual sentiment, does not hide the stink of spiritual resentment. What of your God when you don't get your way?"[ix]

Todd Vickers

What happened to the creeds that have gone out of fashion? It is amazing that such beliefs once obliged people in their daily lives. Perhaps many of our own beliefs today will dissipate, as did the obsolete beliefs from the past. It is something of a pity that our progeny will enjoy the fruits of our mistakes as we benefit from the mistakes of our ancestors. With more scrutiny and less pride, we can enjoy the benefits of abandoning unfounded beliefs before we hand down the learning to our children.

Lamps burn in every house, O
blind one! And you cannot see
them.
One day your eyes shall suddenly be
opened, and you shall see: and the
fetters of death will fall from you.
There is nothing to say or to hear,
there's nothing to do: it is he
who is living, yet dead,
who shall never die again.
Because he lives in solitude, therefore
the Yogi says that his home is far
away.
Your Lord is near: Yet you are climbing
the palm tree to seek Him.

> **The Brahman priest goes from house**
> **to house and initiates people into**
> **faith:**
> **Alas! The true fountain of life is beside**
> **you, and you have set up a stone**
> **to worship.**
> **Kabir says: "I may never express how**
> **sweet my Lord is. Yoga and the**
> **telling of beads, virtue and vice –**
> **these are not to Him.**

SoK PP70

The light is the life that animates us. Life, as an incarnation of matter, emits awareness somehow. Do not confuse what Kabir says with popular ideas about a life after death. Here and now is the time that Kabir points too when he says "the fountain of life is beside you." This present life is different even from our mental representation of it. We wear a mental blindfold when we forget infinite things exist beyond the pale of our thoughts. We are a part of life beginning with the first cells that formed in the primordial waters. That life is like a thread and our particular life is one bead on that thread.

> **Kabir recites couplets**
> **everyday right on time.**
> **The dead do not come back,**
> **no they do not turn around.**

TBoK PP127

Do not sacrifice this life in pursuit of a fiction that promises a reprieve from the fears that we invent. It makes no difference if the future is near or distant. A man in a desert can choose to drink water in fantasy, but his thirst will remain.

> **The moon shines in my body, but**
> **my blind eyes cannot see it:**
> **the moon is within me, and so is the**

sun.

The unstruck drum of Eternity it

sounded in me; but my deaf

ears cannot hear it.

So long as a man clambers for the I and

what is Mine, his works are as naught:

When all love of the I and Mine is

dead, then the work of the Lord

is done.

For work has no other aim than the

getting of knowledge:

When that comes, then work is put

away.

A flower blooms for the fruit: when

the fruit comes, the flower withers. The musk is in the dear,

but it seeks it

not within itself: it wanders in

quest of grass.

SoK PP49

We can make plans and learn things for the sake of creation and discovery. We can't live in the future and nothing separates us from the flowing fountain of this moment. A difference exists between using the mind for something useful and trying to live in the mind, as if that were possible. The obsession with what others might think about us is a uniquely convoluted example. We imagine our self in the thoughts of others and then conceive of what they might be thinking about us. Next, we form our conclusions about what we think they are thinking. This situation can cause misery when we forget that thought is of less substance than a soap bubble. Like a wave on the ocean, thought has its own time and, as it sinks back into the ocean of our awareness, its form is lost completely. Kabir's body was also an event and a temporary part of the flux. Like a stone cast into a vast pool, Kabir's poems are like the ripples that have reached us, several hundred years after the stone sank to the bottom.

If we take life for granted, then we not only avoid the awareness of our own death, but we overestimate the importance of ideas. We say that moonlight exists, but not that the moon is luminous. Sunlight reflects back to us from the moon. Just like this light, awareness reflects back to us in our thoughts even when we are in error. Kabir tells us a secret. The sound of an un-struck drum is silence and, while it is not something we hear, it is behind all we hear. In a quiet mind, the thought of 'I' suddenly goes missing.

> Beware of the world,
> brothers,
> be alert-
> you're being robbed
> while wide-awake.
> Beware of the Vedas,
> brothers,
> be vigilant -
> death will carry you away
> while the guard
> looks on.
> The Neem tree
> becomes the mango tree,
> the mango tree becomes
> the Neem,
> the banana plant
> spreads into a bush -
> the fruit on the coconut palm
> ripens into a berry
> right under your noses,
> you dumb and foolish

rustics!
Hari becomes the sugar
and scatters Himself
in the sand.
No elephant can sift
the crystals from the grains.
Kabir says, renounce
all family, caste, and clan.
Turn into an ant,
Instead -
pick the sugar from the sand
and eat.

TWS PP119

The recognition of our ignorance becomes real knowledge about a fact. Truths are scattered in the sand of innumerable fantasies, lies and distortions that are perpetrated by vested interests. Kabir warns those of us filled with pride, but does not limit this lesson solely to the well-born or those individuals with fortunate circumstances. Anyone can miss something good in the myriad of ideas swirling around or about the good thing. Organic farmers use oil of Neem tree as pesticide. How can Kabir suggest the horribly bitter Neem gets confused with the delicious mango? Such an absurdity calls for a strong example so let us discuss sexuality. We form habits through both repetition and strong sensation. When these two combine, they become even more potent. Our sexual fantasies are often redundant and intense, like many other ideas involving ourselves. Most people approach sexuality limited to the idea that they should imitate other people, art (e.g., romantic literature) or movies (e.g., pornography). Vicarious events and fictions become a point of reference that we can actually feel. We judge actual people in our real lives against fictional events and unrealistic concepts. As such, real lovers seem inferior as a result.

Our own abilities to visualize can blind us to what is in front of our eyes. This type of bad judgment can continue indefinitely. Many good qualities that fall outside of the distorted ideals are debased. Sadly, the losses of these good things may reveal their value to us only when it is too late, if we notice at all. It is tragic to miss something good because we are obsessed with what never happened.

When Kabir recommends abandoning family, caste and religion, he understands that we have nothing binding us to such things. We do not have to live in the abstractions about who we are or what life should be. Therefore, no bonds exist that need to be broken. While we may lose prestige when we embrace autonomy, we will gain access to what life offers us beyond those beliefs.

I'm looking at you,
you're looking somewhere else.
Damn the kind of mind
that's in two places at once.

TBoK PP127

Belief, habit, routine, prejudice and expectation rest on an assumption of an outcome. However, relegating non-redundant circumstances, especially human interactions, to such general inferences, as if we could possibly know the future, is foolish.

I've traveled at home and abroad,
I've tramped the lanes of village after village:
and yet I haven't met a man of discrimination
who can tell things for what they are.

TWS PP186

No illusion can abide without the support of the mind that creates and sustains it. Constant change invites us to focus our faculties. Quieting the mind becomes a break from our routines.

I don't know
what sort of master
you have.

Is he deaf
that the mullah must screech
from the mosque?
Surely He can hear
even the anklets that tinkle
on an ants feet!
You count your beads,
you smear your brow with marks,
you grow your long matted locks.
But deep inside yourself
you carry the vicious dagger
of apostasy-
this isn't the way
to attain the master!

TWS PP202

It seems strange that the denouncer of religion would throw an accusation of apostasy at the faithful. Kabir knows the power of the mind to fabricate enormous falsehoods. It is difficult to fathom how people take for granted such unfounded beliefs, which is why religion is so pretentious. The smoke and mirrors hide the reality. What word would describe a believer rewarded for obedience and punished for noncompliance with shame, scourge, sword and eternal torment after death? Would a God who knows everything need a reminder of his greatness five times a day in prayer or even once per week?

Don't go rushing
to the public meeting place.
In one field are grazing
lion, cow and ass.

TBoK PP107

Rituals are a type of performance art where the participants are both the performers and the spectators. If there were no audience, then the observances would not stand as evidence of piety. Brothels and other dens of *sin* become attractions when religious people travel. The pious often show their true faith when far from home. These people of faith are not losing their devotion when they pay for the services of a prostitute, instead, they are gratifying hidden desires where they will go unnoticed.

Pandit, do some research
and let me know
how to destroy transiency.
Money, religion, pleasure, salvation-
which way do they stay, brother?
North, South, East, West?
In heaven or the underworld?
If Gopal is everywhere, where is hell?
Heaven and hell are for the ignorant,
not for those who know Hari.
The fearful thing that everyone fears,
I don't fear.
I'm not confused about sin and purity,
heaven and hell.
Kabir says, seekers, listen:
Wherever you are
is the entry point.

TBoK PP55

If a man speaks about the most delicious food in the world without having tasted it himself, should we believe him? Why is it that the answer to the previous question does not apply to prophets? To profess an un-provable belief as true, particularly when there are reasons to doubt it, is an infidelity to honesty itself. Our poet does not suggest punishment for these people. The opportunities of the gullible are already sacrificed when they abandon benign and reasonable choices in favor of irrational beliefs. The terrible consequence of credulity the faithful already endure so more punishment exceeds justice.

> **O SERVANT, where dost thou**
> **seek Me?**
> **Lo! I am beside thee.**
> **I am neither in the temple nor in mosque:**
> **I am neither in the Kaaba nor in Kailash:**
> **Neither am I in rites and ceremonies,**
> **nor in Yoga and Renunciation.**
> **If thou art a true seeker, thou shalt at**
> **once see me: meet Me**
> **in a moment of time.**
> **Kabir says, "O Sadhu! God is the**
> **breath of all breath."**

SoK PP45

Life is necessary in all breath. Life is the breath of all breath. We learn to strive to attain our desires. Even the prayers of ascetics seek a paradise. The smallest moment of time is the space between two thoughts. We cannot hold on to the story of ourselves in a smallest space of time, the self narrative does not exist in a tiny moment. It takes time to construct a narrative of our self, and it takes time to infer our experiences are evidence to the self we construct. What Kabir points to cannot be the outcome of work. He speaks of the consciousness that you already have.

> **Three men went on pilgrimage,**
> **jumpy minds and thieving hearts.**
> **Not one sin was taken away;**
> **they piled up nine tons more.**

TBoK PP115

Take the case of '*Man Love Thursday*,' where Islamic men sometimes engage in homosexual activity, in spite of the religious injunction against it. We might call this selective religious compliance. Many religious inconsistencies seem to disappear when washing in the ablution pool. These religious exceptions are not unlike the Catholics who insist that a blowjob is not sex. Even if they admit to a carnal sin, a little donation and confession appeases the priest. Tearing off our hypocritical blindfolds, Kabir points to the tiniest house of time, this moment, where we can live in honesty with ourselves and, if we are fortunate to have such friends, we can share this reality with others.

> **Drop yourself;**
> **worship Hari;**
> **head-to-toe let go**
> **of deformity;**
> **don't be afraid**
> **of life;**
> **the essence**
> **of spirituality.**

TBoK PP105

We miss the inherent values of our present lives when our eyes are fixated on a goal. In all the spiritual practices, Kabir disavows the benefit and future salvation because we can't save any imagined self. The poet says that we will not find a reward in visionary thoughts.

> **This world is completely befooled,**
> **they're missing both yoga and pleasure.**
> **Kabir threshes sesame seeds,**
> **the people thresh chaff.**

TBoK PP125

The spiritual practices that create altered states have a value in that they show us that something exists beyond our expectations. However, the seeker gets tempted to conceive a spiritual self that seems revealed in these efforts. A teacher will profit by encouraging the seeker to maintain and improve this new specter of self. The practitioner is at a loss for money and time, but may not care because the experience itself is gratifying. Remember that what can be attained will be lost.

> **I have wondered at home and abroad,**
> **through alleys, from village to village,**

> **but I never met a fellow**
> **who could winnow,**
> **who could winnow.**

TBoK PP126

If we do not separate the undesirable from what is good, then we will consume them both together. When we learn to sift what is reasonable from foolish, then we also make enemies. When possible, we should distinguish the real advantages from the dubious or false ideas.

> **You gathered a ton of milk**
> **and spoiled it with a drop.**
> **The milk split and soured,**
> **the butter was destroyed.**

TBoK PP113

We transform some things when combining them with others. The value of one thing can mistakenly be associated with something else. Religion offers some things of practical value. Any group of people can accomplish things that an individual would find difficult. I am not referring to superstitious consolation or the prestige of like-minded individuals who flatter each other. If you are God's chosen people, then you and your partisans can enjoy feeling superior. Regardless of the belief, the members of any group have access to a collective pool of experiences and skills. Religion is one way of gathering people together and allows participants to benefit from each other's knowledge. We can receive the benefits of collective shared knowledge apart from religious beliefs. Such benefits cannot endow irrelevant beliefs with credibility.

I heard a minister on the radio listing several compelling facts. He then proceeded to insert a belief that was completely unrelated. Perhaps he had the best of intentions, but he emphasized that his un-testable belief was the peak of human courage. I would suggest credulity is one of the lowest common denominators of humanity and he was exploiting it. To make any idea appealing by endowing it with qualities that it does not possess is a trick. Demagogues and the media that pretends to be news constantly use this trick. Many people think in terms of "all or nothing." They have not learned to grant merit where it is due or withhold it when it is undeserved. Skeptical discrimination enables us to benefit from both the imbecile and genius and not bind ourselves to the folly of either out of gratitude.

We can learn to tie a bowline and this mastery of rope will have countless uses. The knot itself has integrity; it is stronger than any rope and, when properly tied, remains so under stress. We could learn to tie this knot in a Bible school classroom, but the value of this skill does not validate the other beliefs of those teaching. The value is the same if taught by a bigoted, drunken sailor who, by virtue of his occupation, will know how to tie a bowline. It takes someone with integrity to be able to separate what has importance from what does not. Those individuals who share good things may seem credible about many things, when, in fact, they are not. You would not ask a professional cook for advice about the treatment of a brain tumor. We can profit from learning without binding ourselves to the beliefs of those individuals who teach. Let us give credit for sharing something of value: no more and no less.

When we delve into matters of spirituality, absurdities lurk in the unique experiences associated with spiritual practices. Someone who is not familiar with such phenomena and begins to experience them for the first time may be impressed. It is a mistake for skeptics to dismiss these experiences as they are valuable. For example, in vipassana meditation a person watches his own breath, focusing on his belly as it expands and contracts. Vipassana and countless other methods pull our attention away from the habits of our minds. By definition, to be outside of our habitual states is to have an altered or unique experience. Uncommon experiences prove that there exists many states beyond those states familiar to us. On the other hand, those individuals who add "meaning" to these experiences or suggest that, through such practice we can accomplish unlikely things, abase the real value. We should purge altered states of as much superstition as possible just like we boil contaminated water to avoid spreading disease. We hear people describe sensations induced through spiritual practices in vague terms like energy, shakti, spirit, kundalini or chi. When a rational person asks someone who meditates what they mean by these terms, the response will likely be unsatisfying. Without similar experiences, understanding is difficult. The temptation to dismiss the entire event as delusional is misguided. Do not condemn someone for being at a loss for words and describing nerve pain as "ants crawling down their legs." No internal sensation for anyone, including a rationalist, comes with a label! It is not the experience that is delusional or the nebulous descriptive language, but, rather, the arbitrary meaning that both authorities and seekers attach to these experiences. If your wife feels lust for another man, then the fact that you disapprove or are incredulous does not discharge your wife's feelings. Any description, significance or judgment that anyone adds to the circumstance is separate from the wife's lusty feelings.

Most people understand that music affects our subjective experience. Being a musician, I understand some of the subtle ways that sound affects the body-mind. For example, both players and listeners experience changes in feelings due to the tension and release caused by rhythmic phrasing. Add to this experience the elements of melody and harmony and we have a powerfully complex means to altering our states. Many religions appropriate the feelings induced by music by associating the emotion it arouses with its particular doctrine. Nations also use music for the same reason.

Saint Augustine condemned music, but also saw that it could be used for propaganda.[x] The marketplace became more attractive to people than holy places in part because of the arts and music. Apparently, song and color are more fun than threats of damnation. Eventually, it became obvious that the church could use the same means to attract people. Theologians began decorating the churches with many types of art, singing choirs, and pipe organs to attract those hungry for an experience of beauty. The experiences generated through art became associated with the religion.

Some people have dared to suggest that through music we could achieve peace. These people need to familiarize themselves with the history that contradicts this notion. We should note that, after the Catholics introduced music and art into religion, the wars of the 17th century still broke out. Between 1618 and 1648, the followers of Jesus on both sides of the reformation killed eight million people in Europe. Again, the beauty of art may be good without believing the owners of that art are good.

> **When the guru is blind,**
> **what can a student do?**
> **Blind man pushes blind man,**
> **both fall in the well.**

TBoK PP107

Like channeled water becomes more intense when contained and directed, new states of awareness arise by channeling one's attention. We refine concentration through a spiritual practice or ritual. When we focus the vitality that we previously drained into habits, the novel states achieved may astonish us. Unfortunately, the newly accumulated energy can also pour into the imagination. If we understand such an experience, then there is no harm. If we do not understand it, then we can become delusional. I repeat this point because it is exceedingly important. What often passes as spiritual teachings amount to endowing non-typical experiences with meaning and, thus, making fantasy incredibly profitable.

> **Get supplies right here,**
> **the road ahead is bumpy.**
> **They rush to buy heaven**
> **where there's no salesman**

and no shop.

TBoK PP90

A child in the middle of a night-terror believes the monster to be real. He is inconsolable regardless of whether his parents turn on a light and demonstrate the falseness of his belief. Like a child, we are capable of believing images in the mind when we are excited, regardless of evidence to the contrary. The more intense the emotion, the more tempted we are to accept the concept as real. These feelings may be beautiful too, like a swoon induced by lies or the hope of a life beyond this one.

What's the world like?
A flock of sheep.
One falls in the ditch,
the rest jump in.

TBoK PP118

For just one day, let us note every thought we apprehend in our mind on paper. If we were to do this action, we might be astounded as not only would the quantity be vast, but we would also see how much mind stuff appears absurd, repetitive and useless. If you have ever had a song stuck in your head, then you can grasp my meaning. Looking at our habits of mind, let's consider this question. Are we really meeting and relating to others or are we relating to our prejudices about those people? When the answer is the latter we can miss the reality in front of us, which can be like eating rinds, while throwing away the fruit.

We know
what Maya is -
a great robber and thief,
a con-woman
in cahoots with con-men.
She wanders all over the world,
carrying her noose
strung with three strands -

she sits rocking in every place,
using her sweet tongue.
In Keshav's house
she masquerades as Kamala,
in Shiva's mansion
she's Bhavani.
She has settled down
as an idol at the priest's,
she has become
the holy water
at the Pilgrim's destination.
She has planted herself
in the ascetics hut
as an ascetic woman,
in the king's palace
she sits on the throne
as a Queen.
In some homes
she's diamond and Pearl,
in some she's become
a worthless cowrie-shell.
She has moved in
with the common devotee
and become a devotee herself,
she lives with the Muslim
man as his Muslim woman.
Kabir says, listen,
O holy men -
this is the whole
ineffable tale.

TWS PP146

The unscrupulous turn the imagination against those individuals who are vulnerable.

There is a sucker born every minute and two to take him.[xi]

Attributed to P.T. Barnum

**When the learned priests
forget their stuff,
they read the good old Vedas-
without their books,
they don't have a clue
to the secret of things.
When they see
someone's suffering
they pounce on it
with words like karma,
they apply their theories
of the four Ashramas.
They've taught to four ages
the gayatri mantra-
go ask them
whom it has set free.
Whenever they touch someone
they bathe
to purify themselves-
tell them who's really
the inferior one.
They take great pride
in their many good qualities,
but so much vanity
doesn't make them any good.
Only the One**

who's the Destroyer of Pride
can deal with their arrogance.
Give up the thought
of being proud of your birth,
look for the text
of Nirvana.
You'll find
The eternal bodiless
resting place
only when the sapling
has spoilt the seed.

TWS PP149

Sincere people exist who, through religion, seek to help both others and themselves, but they do not find integrity until they mature enough to see through the game. Spirituality has a dark side that we would be fools to ignore. When a holy man flatters someone fortunate that his success is the reward of God, what that person did to achieve that wealth is now sanctioned by a supernatural being, a being who's existence we have no reason to credit. Spiritually flattering people with power is a dangerous game because they use spiritual credibility to justify their actions.

The great are gone in their greatness,
every hair bristling with vanity.
Ignorant of the True Master,
the four castes alike are untouchable.

TWS PP182

Money bolsters self-importance and, with a spiritual explanation for success, wealthy people become shills testifying to the poor to *help* them, convincing the poor that if they give what little they have, they will become worthy of God's abundance. The poor become the victims and the wealthy swell with pride when their success gives them a platform to speak upon.

Kabir, they've spoiled devotion,
bathing stones and pebbles.
The poison's stored inside,
the nectar's poured away.

TBoK PP119

Any doctor who successfully employs a placebo has some understanding of the human ability to create and associate fantastic qualities with sugar pills. Anyone accepted as an authority can direct this power of imagination through suggestion. In the poem above, Kabir refers to a stone idol, but any idolized thing could work like a placebo. A Christian who feels safer wearing a cross is as much an idolater as a Hindu offering a sweet to a statue for the same effect.

The above poem also sheds light on our habits because we may arrest a painful habit by creating a new one. The practice of swapping one habit for another has limits, and spiritual practice is no exception. When we finish our techniques, the habits we wished to avoid may indeed remain. Also, the attempt to overcome one habit with another might consume too much of our attention.

You're a holy man? What are you
if you gab without thinking,
if you stab other beings
with the sword of your tongue?

TBoK PP124

Vast amounts of imaginary nonsense have been peddled to the gullible about religion, spirituality, things that are to be taken on faith. I understand that, eventually, rain will follow a rain dance; however, that result does not prove that the ritual was the cause. Perhaps the greatest perversions, such as cruelty, are worse when they hide in piety. Any mockingbird can repeat words and we can dress an idiot in the garments of a priest, but that doesn't mean that the bird or idiot has earned our deference. We have huge blind spots in our reasoning if we grant authority because of words or robes. A difference exists between doubting our own knowledge and surrendering our judgment over to others. Religion encourages the latter in order to defer to those individuals who wield the power given to them by the suggestible.

Ironically, the people who are seeking money, property, prestige, power or spiritual liberation imagine some satisfaction through these efforts. If we can't satisfy a desire no matter what the accomplishment, then it is a mistake to cling to satisfaction as a motivation. People ignore the fact that everything attained will eventually be lost. Without authorities telling people what to believe, some folks seem lost. Then, when they learn from authority what to do to achieve their desires, they tend to defend the chosen philosophy. They believe or hope that the philosophy they chose is the right one, regardless of the fact that they may have accepted this philosophy for the same reasons that their opponents believe something else.

> **They've taken all the fish**
> **to sell in the Fishers' court.**
> **Your eyes are bloodshot.**
> **Why did you get enmeshed?**

TBoK PP116

Kabir stopped wasting his life chasing the bait offered by the authorities of his time. That's why Kabir's life was his own. Kabir offers disillusionment, a seemingly paltry offering next to the extravagant promises offered by those people society tends to grant influence. People like advertisers and politicians sling bait for the ego, then they cast a huge net and catch many fish.

> **Read, read pandit, make yourself clever.**
> **Does that bring freedom?**
> **Kindly explain.**
> **Where does the supreme being dwell?**
> **In what village? Pandit, tell**
> **his name. Brahma himself**
> **made the Vedas, but he doesn't know**

> the secret of freedom.
> People babble of alms and merit
> but don't hear news
> of their own death.
> One name - unreachably deep.
> Unmoving - the servant Kabir.
> Where an ant can't climb,
> a mustard seed won't sit,
> no going to or from,
> the whole world heads for it.

TBoK PP85

We can watch the activity of our minds like we watch television, but the stories are more subtle because we are the creators. When a habit of the mind catches us, it is not so easy to change the channel in our minds. Our mental world and identity may seem real, but that world of ideas can implode when something shocking happens. Perhaps we received a call that brought death as a message and reminded us that we were mortal. In such moments, the pettiness of our habits is exposed. During a tragedy, things such as winning an argument or watching our favorite TV show or team winning seem less important. Do not be in a hurry to rebuild a banal world when the shocks of such events subside.

> Why run around offering water?
> There's a sea in every house.
> If anyone is thirsty,
> by hook or crook, he'll drink.

TBoK PP91

Again, the error is mistaking the mental schematic of our self for who we actually are. We become willing to doubt our identity when the pain of seeing it threatened becomes excruciating. However, our questioning does not usually lead to recognizing that the identity is conceptual. Our doubts about our ego lead us to imagining how to improve or repair it. Many salespeople make their living selling solutions for imaginary problems, like mice peddling a better mousetrap. Fixing an identity is like bailing water out of a leaking boat. Kabir's words are for the person who is getting tired of bailing.

It is needless to ask of a saint the
caste to which he belongs;
For the priest, the warrior, the tradesmen,
and all the thirty-six castes,
alike are seeking for God.
It is but folly to ask what the caste of
a saint may be;
The Barber has sought God, the washerwoman,
and the carpenter-
Even Raidas was a seeker after God.
The Rishi Swapacha was a tanner by
caste.
Hindus and Muslims alike have
achieved that End, where remains
no mark of distinction.

SoK PP45

Treat a beggar like a prince and he may grow as proud. The rooster struts and announces each sunrise, including the day that the farmer brings an axe. We can struggle to be the top cock, but what does it really matter?

If we stop automatically treating beliefs as facts, the groups from which we spring cannot limit our integrity, Kabir simply gives us back to ourselves and suggests that anyone, even those individuals like himself without any mark of distinction, have access to what is inherently valuable. He ends his prose speaking of an end without a name or distinction. When comparing we say something is like or unlike something else. A yellow snake and a lemon are both alike and unalike; our standards of comparison make the distinction. We create the relationship between things. Take racism as an extreme case to make the point. The absence of distinction Kabir speaks of is not about rejecting our concepts, but rather understanding that we both create or choose the concepts that we then add to circumstances. We are not obligated to limit ourselves to previous concepts. A glass of water may be worthless to a man living by a river. Take the man mentioned previously, put him in the desert without water, and the same glass of water becomes worth all he has in the world.

> **The guru's word is one,**
> **ideas about it endless.**
> **Sages and pandits exhaust themselves,**
> **the Vedas can't touch its limit.**

TBoK PP104

This above poem does not need an explanation.

Meditation

**In the wood where lions
don't tread
and birds don't fly,
Kabir ranges
in empty meditation.**

TBoK PP122

Behind the daily tasks of thinking and doing, we carry inside us the silence where knowledge of self passes like a rustling breeze. In the silence, riches and power are useless. No tyrant or oligarch can pay a sycophant to reflect back to them who they are in this quiescence. Discussing meditation is difficult and leads to being vague.

**Much thinner than water,
subtler than smoke,
swifter than wind,
Kabir's friend.**

TBoK PP115

We assume some conscious being in any of our passing states, yet this consciousness remains inchoate. Sensation and analysis arise, correct or not, in consciousness. Any judgment arises within our conscious neutrality like a swell in the ocean. The quiet vastness inside us that we take for granted whenever there is an object of mind or sense to observe, we can recognize in meditation.

**Drop falling in the ocean-
everyone knows.
Ocean absorbed in the drop-
a rare one knows.**

TBoK PP96

Like canvas without a boundary, our minds contain any image we receive or create. It might be better to say that we can endlessly paint over our previous work, leaving elements that we like and hiding others.

This mental activity is not a problem until we mistake one of these reiterations to be the self. Thought provides the raw materials for the artist. With each stroke of the mind brush our world takes shape, but only as an artistic interpretation. Our creation inspires defensiveness in us when we think that the design means something about, or literally is, the self. Consider how many times we have redefined the self-image. It is as flexible as thought. It is when we try to stabilize some thought and say this is who 'I' am that we feel 'ourselves' threatened by any fact contrary to this thought.

> **One entered all,**
> **all entered that.**
> **Kabir entered knowledge.**
> **No duality.**

TBoK PP121

The past becomes fuzzy or lost in memory as we paint over it with the new mental images. We, should quietly observe how we manufacture these concepts. Let's look closely in order to see the evidence of our own brush strokes in the image. Neither the soup nor the cooking can be the cook. Don't confuse these things and you will pass through the maze of mind.

> **All things are created by the Om;**
> **the love - form is his body.**
> **He is without form, without quality,**
> **without decay:**
> **Seek thou union with him!**
> **But that formless God takes a thousand**
> **forms in the eyes of his creatures:**
> **He is pure and indestructible,**
> **His form is infinite and fathomless,**
> **He dances in rapture, and waves of**
> **form arise from His dance.**
> **The body and the mind cannot contain**

**themselves, when they are touched
by his great joy.
He is immersed in all consciousness, all
joys, and all sorrows;
He has no beginning and no end;
He holds all within his bliss.**

SoK PP74

Conceiving of ourselves seems a natural part of early development and we use such thinking daily. Each time we repeatedly think of 'I', we risk confusing ourselves with this habituated concept. Since we cannot grasp or identify with the consciousness that our thoughts arise within, we seize upon the forms created as either identity or proof of an identity. These ideas take innumerable forms and identification is what Kabir means above when he says God takes a thousand forms. In the above poem replace the word "God" with consciousness and replace "a thousand forms" with the ideas that come and go.

We live in a vastness much broader than our imagined limits. When we let go of our ideas of 'self', we are not bound to the limits of such an arbitrary 'self'. That same 'self' would have an entirely different set of beliefs if we grew up in a different culture with a different religion or system. In particular, the question is not what you would do in this or that circumstance, but what will you choose from the thousands of options available. This access to a greater variety of options from which to choose cannot guarantee an outcome that you want, but makes it so that you are not limited to the options that coincide with what you believe about yourself. We do not need to defer to an authority, an institution or a belief to go beyond the limits of our habits and try something new. We may feel fear, but fear can be imagination ebbing and flowing in the silence. Is it fear based on a real danger or fear of doing something outside of what we have become accustomed?

In terms of any inquiry, we can fall back to the unknown, gather the facts again, which may include knowledge previously unavailable, and begin our discovery anew. From the silence, we can again use our thinking without insisting that it need be perfect. We have no reason to bind who we are to any thought, thus we can abandon any thought including thoughts about the self.

**He is the real Sadhu, who can re-
veal the form of the formless to
the vision of these eyes:
Who teaches the simple way of attaining
Him, that is other than rites
or ceremonies:
Who does not make you close the doors,
and hold the breath, and renounce
the world:
Who makes you perceive the Supreme
Spirit wherever the mind attaches
itself:
Who teaches you to be still in the midst
of all of your activities.
Ever immersed in bliss, having no fear
in his mind, he keeps the spirit of
union in the midst of all enjoyments.
The infinite dwelling of the Infinite
Being is everywhere: in earth,
water, sky, and air:
Firm as a thunderbolt, the seat of
the seeker is established above the
void.
He who is within is without: I see
Him and none else.**

SoK PP101

If we shut our eyes or go blind, we lose our windows to the world, but not the consciousness, the one that registers that the world is now dark. Don't confuse the witness with any thoughts about it.

The above poem has a problem when it says, "having no fear." Either these words are distortions in translation or Kabir made a mistake. In the next verse, he mentions himself experiencing fear. The poet is in danger of a refutation out of his own mouth. The correct interpretation of his phrase "having no fear," should be - that the real Sadhu has no obligation to obey fear or any emotion. This coincides with what the poet says about not losing himself in enjoyments. Pleasures are not his master and, thus, he need not obey them either, but he can experience any feeling of which a human is capable. Regardless of any satisfaction, he doesn't get lost because he is not identifying with the experience.

> **When I am parted from my**
> **Beloved, my heart is full of**
> **misery: I have no comfort in the**
> **day, I have no sleep in the night.**
> **To whom shall I tell my sorrow?**
> **The night is dark; the hours slip by.**
> **Because my Lord is absent, I start**
> **up and tremble with fear.**
> **Kabir says: "listen, my friend! There**
> **is no other satisfaction, save in the**
> **encounter with the Beloved."**

SoK PP98

If we want full access to our faculties and sensitivities, then we must include any experiences that they can sense, including pain. Otherwise, we are in avoidance. Ephemeral emotion does not define us. We remain dangled over the void when we seize an identity and Kabir knows what this fear of losing hold of the identity is like. The moment we grasp

identity, we are under a threat of losing it. This poem points directly
into the void.

My good men,
what comes and goes,
bustling about the world,
is Maya.
The One who's the True Guardian
doesn't inflict
death on anyone-
he doesn't come and go,
he has never moved
from place to place.
Why would He change into
a Fish or Tortoise?
He didn't slay Shankhasura.
He's kind, compassionate-
he doesn't inflict
cruelty on anyone.
Tell me, whom has He ever killed?
He's a maker-
He never went by the name of Varaha.
He didn't lift up the weight of the earth.
These aren't the Lords actions -
the world lies about them.
The one who burst out of a pillar-
everybody believes in him.
He's Narasimha, the Man-Lion,
who tore into Hiranyakashipu's chest
with his claws-
but he isn't the creator.
The Lord didn't assume
the fifty-two forms

that tormented King Bali
in a netherworld -
the one who did that
was Maya.
The whole world bustles about
Indiscriminately -
Maya has deluded the world.
The True Master
wasn't Parashurama,
he didn't slaughter the kshatriyas-
that was a trick
that Maya played.
He doesn't recognize
separation and devotion -
his creatures have invented
these fictions.
The Guardian of the universe
wasn't the one
who married Sita,
He didn't build the bridge across the sea
with rocks and stones.
That was merely
the master of Raghu's clan,
who's commemorated for such deeds-
anyone who memorializes him
as though he were the Lord
is a blind man.
The creator wasn't the cowherd
who consorted with those cowgirls-
he didn't go to Gokul,
he didn't murder Kamsa.
The masters gracious to everyone-

he hasn't been

the winner or loser

in any war.

The creator isn't the one

who's called the Buddha,

he didn't destroy the asuras.

Those who're ignorant

are deluded about the world-

Maya has deluded the world.

The creator isn't the one

who'll become Kalki,

he won't be the future killer

of Kaligrahi.

Maya's the one

who has created this confusion-

she has impeded

the true renouncer,

the faithful wife.

For those who worship the Master

the ten avatars

are a masterful illusion

Kabir says, listen,

O saintly men-

What springs to life

And expends itself

Is utterly different from Him.

TWS PP164

Do not limit the criticism to the sages and gods that Kabir has named. Let us not spare our favorite saints. We should not leave all of the work to a man long dead.

Our thoughts *about* the world complicate many things. We endow people and things with qualities they don't have and also miss qualities that they do possess. Any event in nature that we value unto itself, like a human being, we can also value exclusively as a means to some other end. We're tempted to value people exclusively for what they can do for us. It is sad that many people will offer a gesture of respect for the dead when, in life, they valued the same carcass only by its usefulness. In death, we tend to acknowledge the inherent value of people; it is both unkind and foolish not to do so when they are alive. We even make the same mistake with ourselves. Perhaps how we understand ourselves explains our disregard of others. If we believe that we only exist to maintain our egos, then, of course, we expect others to do the same for us and for themselves.

> **What can the poor road do?**
> **The travelers don't know where they are going.**
> **Leaving their own path,**
> **they stumble from wasteland to wasteland.**

TBoK PP112

Most people seek the next thing that promises satisfaction. Each material or spiritual path has joys and pains, but it is the belief that our circumstances define us that haunts our waking hours. For example, take a husband or wife. The person may *say* that his or her spouse is not a means for ego fulfillment, but we have a test for such things. Let the spouse fuck someone else and then see what the husband or wife says. Words are often like flatulence in the wind; it emits a noise and raises the eyebrows of those individuals who hear it.

Some people argue that sexual fidelity is something good beyond being a means. I admit that *might* be so, but one test of faithfulness is in the secrets that people keep from their partners. There are many men who will not be sexual their wives but constantly masturbate to pornography. Perhaps a Machiavellian spouse finds that the truth about affairs or prostitutes does not serve his or her purposes and, thus, abandons truth telling. Unless you catch someone in a lie, it is difficult to distinguish someone cunning from one who is faithful.

> **Praise the diamond that survives**
> **a reign of blows.**
> **When a phony man is tested**
> **his badness shows.**

TBoK PP108

Anyone can seem enlightened in the midst of a windfall and agreeable circumstances. When the storm hits and some people exploit others to achieve an end, you will know what Kabir means.

> **Mind and Maya are one,**
> **Maya fuses with the mind.**
> **The three worlds are plunged into delusions.**
> **To whom I can explain this?**

TWS PP181

If someone or something we desire is beyond our means to grasp, then that is only one passing circumstance. However, what we think about that situation can extend indefinitely. We may think it means something about us, that we are too fat, poor or ugly. We may imagine that, by doing something different, we might have succeeded. Our concepts about any event are *not* what actually happened any more than a concept of a woman or man could love us. The diversions of the mind are like carnival peep shows, but consciousness waits, while we are distracted. Even if we are spending too much time on the carnival amusements, our awareness awaits in the background no matter how stupid we are. Awareness itself is more loyal than any spouse and that is why we take it for granted.

> **O BROTHER, my heart yearns for**
> **that true Guru, who fills the cup**
> **of true love, and drinks of it him-**
> **self, and then offers it to me.**
> **He removes the veil from the eyes, and**
> **gives the true Vision of Brahma:**
> **He reveals the worlds in him, and**

> makes me to hear the Unstruck
> Music:
> He shows joy and sorrow to be one:
> He fills all utterance with love.
> Kabir says: "Verily he has no fear,
> who has such a Guru to lead him
> to the shelter of safety!"

SoK PP71

The fortunate one not only gives love, but takes it as well. The true guru reveals that the world of the mind arises in him just as it does in everyone. The difference is that, for the true guru, thoughts are not an identity. All of his thoughts are hypothetical. The true guru points to the unstruck music, meaning silence, present in the melody, rhythm and harmony; the silence behind that sound, the silence between two thoughts. To the awakened one happiness, grief and any experience pass like notes of music in a song, like weather in the vast sky. Our individual experiences, like our lovers and our own bodies, are passing events in a long chain of life.

The mistake about denying fear occurs again in the poem above. Still the one who realizes that identity is a fiction need not reject fear because fear is not a master, but a servant. We can disobey our servant.

> Receive that word from which
> the Universe springith!
> That word is the Guru; I have heard
> it, and become the disciple.
> How many are there who know the
> meaning of that word?
> O Sadhu! Practice that word!
> The Vedas and the Puranas proclaim it,
> The world is established in it,
> The Rishi's and devotees speak of it:
> But none knows the mystery of the

word.
The householder leaves his house when
he hears it,
The ascetic comes back to love when
he hears it,
The six philosophies expound it,
The Spirit of Renunciation points to
that Word,
From that Word the world-form has
sprung,
That word reveals all.
Kabir says: "But who knows whence
the Word comith?"

SoK PP102

Before we speak an experience, we feel a sensation. It flashes in us without a name. Not that we call sadness by its name. We feel a sensation and then call it sadness. The same is true of any feeling. The events we illustrate by clothing them in words are new experiences even though the words we use are threadbare from stretching them too tight or hanging them too loosely. What we describe to people is not exactly the feeling we have and we view these feelings through our preconceived ideas.

Imagine three people fully aware that they are unable to escape from a burning building: a Hindu, Christian and skeptic. They all cry out for help. Their ordinary habits of mind wouldn't function and, unless I miss my guess, they would be in an altered state. Suddenly, a fireman breaks through the wall and saves them. Before their ordinary routines of thought reemerged, they would be in a unique state of mind. If someone asked them to describe what they were feeling, they would probably scan their internal dictionary for words. The word 'gratitude' might come, but they also felt gratitude when their grandfathers gave them birthday money, so this word is not exactly what they mean. The Hindu might give thanks to Krishna for the rescuer, a Christian might thank Jesus and the skeptic might say that he has no words to express how thankful he is, while they are all trying to describe a similar feeling. Later, if asked by intimate friends to try to describe their feelings, they might say that it's impossible. However, the Hindu might say, "I felt the Shakti moving in me like never before;" the Christian might say, "I felt touched by the Lord;" and the skeptic might say "my whole nervous system was *on fire* with indescribable sensations."

All of our descriptions are approximations and the words that we use are used because we lack better words. They serve their purposes, but fall short, particularly when describing subjective experiences. We try to reach out to others to relate to them, but our words falter. The attempt to say something truer involves trial and error to find a suitable word. The space between our consciousness of the feeling and the more or less flawed word we choose is the unarticulated alive feeling and we do not want to lose sight of this experience just because we have located and chosen some label. Do not let our prejudiced comparisons, distinctions and conclusions become limits. Let us not forget that we leave a great deal out of our descriptions. Let's see the limits and do the best we can to represent our universe in words. Let us not pretend that we don't change things trying to communicate. We may try to create the world with words, but, as Kabir points out in the poem above, who knows "whence the word cometh?" Let's not forget the consciousness that is a necessary part of experience.

On this tree is a bird: it dances

in the joy of life.

None knows where it is: and who

knows what the burden of its

music may be?

Where the branches throw a deep

shade, there does it have its nest:

and it comes in the evening and
flies away in the morning, and says
not a word of that which it means.
None tell me of this bird that sings
within me.
It is neither colored nor colorless:
it has neither form nor outline:
it sits in the shadow of love.
It dwells within the unattainable, the
infinite, and the eternal; and no
one marks when it comes and goes.
Kabir says: "O brother Sadhu! Deep is the mystery.
Let wise men seek
to know where rests that bird.

SoK PP78

You will find the deepest shade in a quiet mind, when one slips beyond dreams into the silence of deep sleep yet remaining conscious. Every morning, we either come out of the darkness into a dream or wake up into our work-a-day world. The 'I' thought arises and, with it, the quiet seems lost. Even in the midst of tortured and deluded thinking, the song of silence exists in the background. Reason becomes one wing on Kabir's bird and intuition the other. Both wings work on the body of the bird capable of observing the world. *As a unified organism,* this bird flies into the vast sky of consciousness. The tree the bird sits in is our life and it exists right now.

Between the conscious and unconscious, the
mind has put up a swing:
all earth creatures, even the supernovas,
sway between these two trees,
and it never winds down.
Angels, animals, humans, insects by the million, also
the wheeling sun and moon; ages go by, and it goes on.

**Everything is swinging: Heaven, earth, water, fire,
and the secret one slowly growing a body.
Kabir saw that for fifteen seconds, and it made him a
servant for life.**

TKB PP11

Our experiences and our words describing them are a swing from the unconscious to the conscious. On a sunny spring day, if we become aware of the birds singing we can enjoy what we call beauty. It is possible the bird songs were present before we noticed. If we felt occupied with other matters, we could've remained unconscious of the bird songs. In experience, we swing from unconscious to conscious, from something unnoticed to a sensation to a name and then that naming can even alter or create a different sensation.

Like one grape growing on a vine that extends back to the first germs of life we are part of one continuing, unfolding, discovering, reproducing, adapting and withering life. We get lost thinking life is in us when, in fact, it is the other way around. This is like mistaking the grape as a mere individual, but it is really part of a whole vine with countless others. Inside the grape, a germ of that same life exists for the sake of continuance.

"We regard the solar system, or the Earth, or a continent, or a mountain, or a stone on that mountain, or an atom in that stone, each as an *object*, according to our need. Our distinctions and relations are the pattern of our uses which we stamp upon the face of unity. The forms of our spatial demarcations are entirely functional; they have no structural reality. Our *atom*, for instance, only exists by virtue of its effects upon every other atom in the universe, and is itself but the resultant in a given point of view, of all the forces in the universe. The atom and the universe are not separable entities; our distinction between the one and the other is but an abstractional manipulation."[xii]

Robert Briffault

The nameless conscious awareness that any naming arises from remains unarticulated in every truth, in any lie and in all error. Consciousness is tacit in the midst of experience, yet often unnoticed. As in dreamless sleep, who noticed to give the description of no time? When Kabir saw this consciousness, he understood that the activity of thought and the senses are not the self. From that moment on, he was never obliged to serve identity as a master.

See the diver's courage:
plunges in cold depths,
rushes past obstacles,
brings back the pearl.

TBoK PP125

Kabir's pearl is not an experience; it is the recognition that you are not your experiences. This inquiry into the self doesn't offer consolation. Anything in the mind can vanish like smoke. Many people who engage in rituals, meditate and enjoy the ephemeral feelings and buzzes that result are often tempted to defer to some teacher, guru or authority to name and define these experiences. Other people who dislike such experiences add a negative connotation to them. Both sets of individuals are doing the same thing for they are adding meaning to sensation. Such added implications could never be proven true or false. Just rush past that added meaning and bring back the pearl.

There is a Secret One inside us;
the planets in all the galaxies
pass through his hands like beads.
That is a string of beads one should look at with
luminous eyes.

TKB PP29

The whole of existence gets portrayed in our experience and words, some say beautiful, others say ugly, and countless others use different gradations of interpretation. We have no need to take a vow of silence to guard against error, just remember what words are and what they are not as they are only symbols. Then, we see those beads as both experiences and words that we string together with the maturity of one unthreatened by the limitations of words and experiences.

It is time to put up a love swing!
Tie the body and then tie the mind so that they
swing between the arms of the Secret One you
love,
Bring the water that falls from the clouds to your eyes,
and cover yourself inside entirely with the shadow of night.
Bring your face up close to his ear,
and then talk only about what you want deeply to
happen. Kabir says: Listen to me, brother, bring the shape,
face, and odor of the Holy One inside you.

TKB PP36

His verse calls for us to come home and listen to the song of ourselves like notes of music in a deeply calm evening. Let's come without the ideas of ourselves that we put on as clothes and be naked. Just a few moments in the absence of thought and we are covered in the darkness of night. Like a deep sleep, we enter into a paradox of both being and not being.

O HOW may I ever express that
secret word?
O how can I say He is not like this, and
He is like that?
If I say that He is within me, the universe
is ashamed:
if I say that He is without me, it is

> falsehood.
> He makes the inner and the outer
> worlds to be indivisibly one;
> The conscious and the unconscious,
> both are His footstools.
> He is neither manifest nor hidden, He
> is neither revealed nor unrevealed:
> There are no words to tell that which
> He is.

SoK PP52

So many charlatans have hidden behind mystery, but we all know this ordinary limitation. When we look closely, we see no one accurately describes anything, some depictions are just better than others. If we tried to verbalize our greatest joys or pains, then how doubtful would our own choice of language seem to us? We would hesitate still further before believing the listener understood our meaning. In admitting his own limits, Kabir strips us of our unwarranted confidence and then goads us on in our own self inquiry.

> There's a mirror in your heart,
> but you can't endure the sight
> of your face in it: you can bear to look
> only when you've ceased to doubt.

TWS PP179

We endure countless futile efforts to stabilize an ephemeral self rather than face the mirror of death. The yawning grave has the power to expose what is trivial by reflecting a reality that we need not doubt. Our hearts rip open when gazing at the most trustworthy glimpse of the future. Like hidden treasure, many unconsidered choices lay in the awesome recognition of mortality. The unavoidable approach of death promises to destroy our imagined futures. Beware the charlatans who will try to rob us of the gift with a promise of existence beyond this life.

Baited with our unfulfilled desires, this trap often proves too tempting and we turn away from the only flawless mirror.

> "One way a hunter can trap a monkey is to secure a gourd to a tree and then place something sweet or shiny in the gourd while a monkey watches, then the hunter leaves. The poor monkey just cannot stand not possessing the bait and will reach into the gourd and grasp it, but as his fist closes around the bait it becomes too big to remove it from the opening of the gourd and he is trapped. The monkey could have his freedom if he would let go but he will not. When the hunter comes, the monkey will freak out and screech but still he will not let go. Thus, the slaughter of the monkey.
>
> This is a better definition of Karma than any I have ever seen. The hunter is karma, the gourd is like the events of life, the monkey is the mind, the grasped object is 'identity' and the grasping is desire. When we identify with events, experiences, and thought then we are no different than this monkey." [xiii]

Todd Vickers

**Within the heart a mirror
but no face shows.
You'll see the face when your heart's
doubleness goes.**

TBoK PP92

Dogma hides doubt and demands that a belief must be true. To believe we will overcome doubt with faith becomes a vicious mistake. The more we pretend a perfect assurance of our knowledge, the more we hold our suspicions at a distance. We seek out authorities who offer guarantees of a future life and this seeking exposes our doubts and our fear of death. Even worse, unworthy authorities encourage us to imagine awful consequences for disobedience to customs. If our ancestors obeyed such authority without question, human progress would not have grown beyond where such obedience began. The struggle to live better drives us toward the limits of any custom. The fact of progress, in opposition to dogma imposed by the powerful, does not stop the powerful from seeking compliant followers. Dare to look into the mirror of silence, in that little death, you will see the ideas of self evaporate. This clarity offers disillusionment, of not only our future, but also of the fanciful present.

He has no shape or line,
no flesh, no base.
In the middle of the sky-temple,
see the bodiless man.

TBoK PP130

Regardless of what we think or believe, when sinking into the void, identification does not matter. Who are we when we stop imagining who we are? New facts penetrate our resistance and force us out of habits and beliefs. Human progress might be far less were it not for these shocks. Looking to history, we see huge changes between the past and present, but we must remain almost blind, looking beyond what we already know.

Good words, bad words,
back-and-forth goes the tongue.
Mind gives a hit: this way and that.
It's death behind the swing.

TBoK PP98

While considering good and bad words, remember the unrealizable promises of spiritual guides, who claim good intentions and hover around people in agony. These spiritual authorities infantilize people, giving them relics, scriptures, prayers and beliefs to cling to for safety as a child clutches a teddy bear. People who mollify others destroy the opportunity for people to adapt to the circumstances they actually face. Lies are often more pleasant then the truth and people who prefer to be placated will find plenty of shysters willing to provide the services, as if people live better by believing something more agreeable than the facts.

Our pending death suggests the shattering of our identity one way or another. Why wait for death to bring that gift when we can enjoy it in life? Let us love, even as we daily face the mirror of doom. Do not turn away because the reality can help us to live better. We can gaze into this abyss before the fire of change envelopes our ideas of self. If we are willing, then we can let identity go of our own volition, rather than having it torn away. Then, we can face changes in life as conscious, feeling creatures with real choices.

> **"The small ruby everyone wants has fallen out on**
> **the road.**
> **Some think it is east of us, others west of us.**
> **Some say, "among primitive earth rocks," others, "in**
> **the deep waters."**
> **Kabir's instinct told him it was inside, and what it**
> **was worth,**
> **and he wrapped it up carefully in his heart cloth."**
>
> TKB PP44

People want to slake their thirst and yearn for things that promise satisfaction. The faith of the spiritual seeker, like the materialist, generally revolves around the idea that some attainment will yield a permanent equanimity. We should have learned long ago from our own experiences that this idea is folly.

> **Where buyers swarm, I'm not;**
> **where I am, there's no buyer.**
> **Without awareness they wander,**
> **plucking at shadows of the world.**
>
> TBoK PP123

Credulous people continually face a deluge of fictionalized lifestyles as propaganda for products, services and *ideas* that *suggest* the cure for discontent. Those interested sellers exploit people's hopes through advertisements by showing paid actors as contented people living fictional lives, as if some particular satisfaction can succeed where many others previously failed. Ironically, the hucksters will likely spend the profits from this shell game chasing their own tails as victims of a similar swindle.

Kabir sees that he cannot actualize any concept of self by acquiring or renouncing any object or experience because the self concept never really existed as anything outside the mind. You cannot really ride the idea of a motorcycle. Kabir unwraps and displays the jewel, while people pass by without seeing any value. He cannot even give it away.

> **He is dear to me indeed who can**
> **call back a wanderer to his**
> **home. In the home is the true**
> **union, in the home is enjoyment of**
> **life: why should I forsake my**
> **home and wonder in the forest?**
> **If Brahma helps me to realize**
> **truth, verily I will find both**
> **bondage and deliverance in home.**
> **He is dear to me indeed who has power**
> **to dive deep into Brahma; whose**
> **mind loses itself with ease in His**
> **contemplation.**
> **He is dear to me who knows Brahma,**
> **and can dwell on his supreme**
> **truth in meditation; and who can**
> **play the melody of the infinite by**
> **uniting love and renunciation in life.**
> **Kabir says: "the home is the abiding**

**place; in the home is reality; the
home helps to attain Him Who is
real. So stay where you are, and all
things shall come to you in time."**

SoK PP87

In the previous poem, Kabir says that we will "find both bondage and deliverance in home," a seeming contradiction. What he means is that we cannot escape from circumstances and that is why the one who renounces earthly experience is wrong. However, if we emancipate ourselves from identification with circumstances, we escape the trap of the materialist. While we are alive, our real homes are our own living, feeling, and cognizing beings. Our faculties, including sensitivity, have evolved to be of a benefit to us. Our capacity for making mistakes is not the real problem of human misery. We can discover our faults as we grope through trial and error toward a greater understanding of the truth; like a composer creates music, we create the songs of our lives.

The only renunciation with any integrity is non-identification with experience. If you do not quite understand what I mean by non-identified, then you may understand that self cannot be the thoughts that come and go. If we recognize this fact, then we will not insist that the events and trials of life must prove or stabilize such ideas. We understand the futility of asking "but what if that hadn't happened," and we begin living and reasoning based on the choices offered by the events.

What does the poet mean when he says "all things will come to us in time"? Our choices are not just this or that; we are not limited to only black or white. We can experiment with things, outside of any past description of ourselves. As we step outside our mental habits, we change our lives and make new mistakes. We also make new discoveries beyond anything we possibly imagined before. Yet, if we remain in bondage to habits of the mind, then we will probably miss many opportunities. We have many choices available to us wherever we go, but, by clinging to a sense of self, we limit our options.

Where speech was: the syllable.
Where the syllable was: a firm mind.
Speech and silence are the same.
A knower is hard to find.

TBoK PP113

We create the meaning we add to any symbol called a word. Conscious thought or speech is different than a parrot that imitates without understanding, but, like the bird, we can also talk habitually, moving our mouths unconsciously like we are chewing gum.

The creations of our minds are like statues of gold, we can reform the ideas by subjecting them to the heat of scrutiny. We can change the form, yet the gold is the same. Let the artistry come forth from our desire to have our words more accurately represent the truth.

The body's a ship,
the mind's a Crow that flies a million miles.
Sometimes it roams on the boundless sea,
sometimes it shoots to the sky.

TBoK PP119

We can imagine not only a self, but anticipate situations for that unreal self in a time to come. The mind cannot go beyond its own scope. Still, we can think anything within the limits of our capacity and mistake ideas as facts, and, worse, we can distort the facts to protect our beliefs.

If you're true, a curse can't reach you
and death can't eat you.
Walking from truth to truth
what can destroy you?

TBoK PP125

It might seem strange that the poet, who elsewhere acknowledges death without any future life, would say such a thing. He does not mean our deaths will not come. He is talking about the fear of dying while we are alive. When we feel consumed by the fear of death, it motivates us to believe many doubtful things. The grave beckons us eventually and, with that unavoidable predator death always hunting, we can't justify blindly obeying the fear as if we could ultimately escape it. Do not let the fear of death rob us of our life.

> **When nothing was made,**
> **no earth or water,**
> **no creator or destroyer-**
> **Kabir speaks of *then*.**

TBoK PP113

In meditation, we lose the fear of ourselves. Each time we descend into silence, our beliefs about the world go missing. There is no reason to grieve the loss of a treasure that we never possessed. We conceptualize death along with a self that becomes threatened by reality. The interaction between these two ideas *self* and *death* takes us deeper into the mind. We are literally thinking about something else that we are thinking about. For example, someone imagines leaving a lover and then he imagines nobody else wanting him, which causes him to feel inferior. Then, he imagines dying alone and miserable. The previous train of thought can become a source of motivation to stay in a destructive relationship. Regardless of how much we try, we can't really know the future in a particularly relevant sense unless we're discussing death. To be in the thrall of miseries that have not happened is to bind oneself with imagination.

> **To what shore would you cross, o**
> **my heart? There is no traveler**
> **before you, there is no road:**
> **Where is the movement, where is the**
> **rest on that shore?**
> **There is no water; no boat, no boat-**
> **man, is there;**

> There is not so much as a rope to tow
> the boat, nor a man to draw it.
> No earth, no sky, no time, no thing, is
> there: no shore, no ford !
> There is neither body nor mind:
> and where is the place that shall
> still the thirst of your soul? You
> shall find naught in that emptiness.
> Be strong, and enter into your own
> body: for there your foothold is
> firm. Consider it well o my
> heart! Go not elsewhere.
> Kabir says "put all imaginations
> away, and stand fast in that which
> you are."

SoK PP69

This song speaks to everyone who has ever suffered the discontent of having desire fulfilled followed by another yearning. He knows the curse of believing that, if we could only satisfy some unfulfilled want, then we would come to rest. In the moment of satisfaction, we seem free from desire, this suggests that freedom from desire is the real longing. Kabir points to the meditation where nothing abides in the silence.

Have the people we admire most crossed the river or do we imagine them on the other shore? Look closer. Are they bound in an endless pursuit of desires? Do they also complain when their master, the mind, beats them? Even the ascetic hankers for liberation. We associate happiness with the events that coincide with pleasures and seem to be its cause. If we believe that we must chase the circumstances that will give us *brief* glimpses of easefulness in order to have a "real" life, then we are slaves to the fickle events of life that we cannot control.

Stop believing that some experience of joy, if maintained, would be the end of discontent. Regardless of our gratification, the journey to cross the river noted by Kabir drags on. We can always excuse our failure to arrive on the other shore. Our wishes and hopes open the door to the salesmen hawking pleasures of the spirit and, these "experts" use their profits to try to get themselves to that other shore.

Step outside of your imagination and answer Kabir's question. Who do you know that has found rest? The answer goes against the long habituated beliefs that we have learned through the imitation of others who hold sway. I am not saying that we should avoid desire. The satisfaction of desire cannot be what we imagine. We miss the obvious when our minds envision others at rest on that other shore. That fictional narrative pretends to be proof that people with more wealth, beauty and ornaments of prestige do succeed in crossing. We imagine ourselves on that shore as we see the *lucky* ones in our mind. Kabir shows this image to be unreal. The attempt to cross the river and secure a sense of self that is unreal is an exercise in futility.

We cannot pour coffee into a cup of thought. Let's take a moment of silence when thought and imagination ceases and notice that we do not cease to be. Only thought is absent. Self-realization can be none other than the recognition of this awareness without a name. We shall not find the ego or anything in a quiet mind. In the poem above, he says "...put all imaginations away, and stand fast in that which you are." Seeing through the mists, he points the way to inquiry, which gives courage. Kabir provokes inquiry into this being where the foothold is firm because we have never been anywhere the unarticulated self does not go with us.

> **The self forgets itself**
> **as a frantic dog in a glass temple**
> **barks himself to death;**
> **as a lion, seeing a form in the well,**
> **leaps on the image;**

as a rutting elephant sticks his tusk
in a crystal boulder.
The monkey has his fist full of sweets
and won't let go. So
from house to house
he gibbers.
Kabir says, parrot-on-a-poll:
who has caught you?

TBoK PP67

We are not in any danger unless we mistake thought for who we are. Then, the dog will bark. The capacity for our minds to suggest alternative actions or choices is, itself, not a problem. However, once we treat some idea as a fact just because we think it, we are tortured: "If you only would've stayed..." or "if you would've left..." Then, we imagine a result where we would have been satisfied had we made a different choice. Life goes by while we languish in such mental incontinence; we are swinging back and forth in the polarities, obsessing on the emotion induced. Eventually, death will bring peace by stopping the pendulum, but quieting the mind is easier. We have many more choices to explore when we emancipate ourselves from the fictional outcomes suggested in our minds.

The world drowned
in an eye-shadow house,
homage to the one
who can get in and out.

TBoK PP116

Notice the advice is to move both in and out of the illusions we create. Our thoughts offer more temptations than the most ornate bordello. If we fear to go into the mind, then we become ineffective to others and ourselves. We must remember that the fire that warms the hearth on a cold night can burn down the house and even the neighborhood. How many women became ashes on the wind because the credulous believed in witches? Therefore, we should heed the warning and not take lightly the faculties of thought.

Open your eyes of love, and see
Him who pervades this world!
consider it well, and know that
this is your own country.
When you meet the true Guru,
He will awaken your heart:
He will tell you the secret of love and
detachment, and then you will
know indeed that He transcends
this universe.
This world is the City of Truth, it's
maze of paths enchants the heart:
We can reach the goal without crossing
the road, such is the sport unending.
Where the ring of manifold joys ever
dances about Him, there is the
sport of Eternal Bliss.
When we know this, then all our
receiving and renouncing is over;
Thenceforth the heat of having shall
never scorch us more.
He is the Ultimate Rest unbounded:
He has spread His form of love throughout all the world.
From that Ray which is Truth, streams
of new forms are perpetually spring-
ing: and He pervades those forms.
All the gardens and groves and bowers
are abounding with blossom; and
the air breaks forth into ripples

of joy.
There the swan plays a wonderful game,
There the Unstruck Music eddies
around the Infinite One;
There in the midst of the Throne of the
Unheld is shining, whereon the great Being sits-
Millions of suns are shamed by the
radiance of a single hair of His body.
On the harp of the road
what true melodies are being sounded! and
it's notes pierce the heart:
There the Eternal Fountain is playing
its endless life-streams of birth
and death.
They call Him Emptiness who is the
Truth of truths, in Whom all
truths are stored!
There within Him creation goes forward, which is beyond all philosophy;
for philosophy cannot attain
to him:
There is an endless world, O my
Brother! There is the Nameless Being, of whom naught can
be said.
Only he knows it who has reached that
region: it is other than all that
is heard and said.
No form, no body, no length, no
breadth is seen there: how can I
tell you that which it is?
He comes to the Path of the Infinite

**on whom the grace of the Lord
descends: he is freed from births
and deaths who attains to Him.
Kabir says: "it cannot be told by the
words of the mouth, it cannot be
written on paper:
It is like a dumb person who tastes a
sweet thing - how shall it be explained?"**

SoK PP118

Kabir gives us many descriptions. We have to be exceptionally clear because what Kabir says can be lost in the poetic and esoteric jargon. Let's look again at what Kabir includes as qualities of the word 'He.' He is ultimate rest unbounded and he pervades this world and your own country and the city of truth. The unbounded maze is another way to say mind and He too abides there as well as in emptiness. Kabir goes on to say He enchants the heart and He is where we need not cross a road to reach and so on. If we think of Kabir's description of 'He' as anything other than consciousness, it turns his words into twaddle.

**Broadcast, O mullah,
your merciful call to prayer-
you yourself are a mosque
with ten doors.
Make your mind your Mecca,
your body, the Ka'aba-
your self itself
is the supreme Master.
In the name of Allah, sacrifice
your anger, error, impurity-
chew up your senses,
become a patient man.
The Lord of the Hindus and Turks
is one and the same-**

> why become a mullah,
> why become a sheik?
> Kabir says, brother,
> I've gone crazy-
> quietly, quietly, like a thief,
> my mind has slipped into the simple state.

TWS PP121

These observations are dangerous and heretical. Our tenderhearted poet sees the error of believing in fantasies. Kabir's love of people made him willing to risk the rage of the faithful in order to help end delusion. His words beckon all of us, his extended family toward the simple state: the quiescence.

> When at last you are come to the
> ocean of happiness, do not go
> back thirsty.
> Wake, foolish man! For death stalks
> you. Here is pure water before
> you; drink it at every breath.
> Do not follow the Mirage on foot, but
> thirst for the nectar;
> Duruva, Prahald, and Shukadeva have
> drunk of it, and also Raidas has
> tasted it:
> The Saints are drunk with love, their
> thirst is for love.
> Kabir says: "listen to me, brother!
> The nest of fear is broken.
> Not for a moment have you come face
> To face with the world:
> You are weaving your bondage of
> falsehood, your words are full of
> deception:

**With a load of desires which you hold
on your head, how can you be
light?
Kabir says: "keep within you truth,
detachment, and love.**

SoK PP105

We view this world through assumptions and beliefs. Realizing that what we see must be different from reality can be difficult to understand. What this poet sensed about five centuries ago, we can clarify in a more cogent way today by taking our beliefs to be good, bad or false. We improve these ideas over time through trial and error. Kabir noticed this long before Emanuel Kant reckoned the unbridgeable distance between things in themselves[xiv] and things in our mind. Not for a moment have we come face-to-face with the world. The world cannot be what we think about it.

Death

The night's gone:
don't let the day go by, too.
The bumblebees have left:
the cranes have arrived, alighted.
The soul, a young girl,
trembles, thinking:
I don't know
what my husband's going to do.
Water won't keep
in a jar of unbaked clay.
The swan has flown away:
the body wilts.
Kabir says:
My arms ache
from scaring off the crows.
This tale has reached its end.

TWS PP116

Like yesterday's dusk, years go by, and the curtain of the unknown envelops us. Someone we know disappears forever and calls attention to our own fate. Some people aroused by circumstances become more conscious, less automatic. However, a shock may only temporarily awaken us out of the habits of mind, time passes, again the trivial amusements and disputes gain in importance. We take many things for granted in the avoidance of our mortality. The crows have learned to both steal from the living garden and feed off death. Our poet cannot hide his weariness from the effort spent trying to save the harvest from these scavengers.

We talk of death like virgins murmur of sex, pretending to know. Our fantasies became a solace. Our faith rests upon others agreeing when judging the evidence we invent, as if consensus could turn cow shit into curry. We turn away from life and take refuge in concepts.

Alongside the facts, doubt deserves reverence as something sacred. It protects us from illusions. A woman developed a strange blemish on her nose. Previously, she had mentioned to me that her mother died of skin cancer. When alone, I asked her about the blotch. She dismissed the implication confidently. I insisted that she have the spot looked at by a doctor. She mentioned a similar pleading from her family. She seemed to be avoiding the action out of fear. Not knowing the best course, I improvised. With a raised voice, I declared her stupid and demanded that she quit fucking around and go to the doctor. Her initial response did not strike me as positive, but she did get a biopsy, which revealed an aggressive cancer growing inward. The fast tracked surgery removed the tumor without destroying her face.

Anyone can be enticed and blinded by self-consoling thoughts. Do not confuse this action with being dumb. There is no motivation for real stupidity; it is innocent. On the other hand, *ignoring* something is an act of volition and requires effort, even sophistication. Ignorance focuses on both the concepts in the mind and the emotions generated to obscure facts. It may be possible for a stupid person to grasp what he was missing. The willfully ignorant may not be so lucky.

It surprises Kabir how we can agitate ourselves over the trivial when our hair will burn and our bones will become tasty to crows. One way or another, we disintegrate. To measure our lives by our ideas instead of testing our beliefs against the realities of life remains a source of misery today. We act as if death has an obligation to be what we visualize it to be. Arrogant salesmen profit by teaching people to discard both their reason and sensuality in this life to pursue rewards after death. Optimism about a dubious future in a crowd of like-minded others is common.

Plant a tiny grain,
harvest eighty kilos.

> **Death has pitched his tent.**
> **He walks, night and morning.**
> **Plant eighty kilos,**
> **harvest not a grain.**
> **No one hears my words.**
> **In the end, they go out**
> **ruined.**

TBoK PP105

All our moments flow toward the destroyer. Even advocates of the "be here now" tradition can miss the point. To suppose what the world would be like if we were truly present in it, this fiction substituted one imagination for another and misses the point. It seems trivial to say a lifetime is a chain of moments that we can miss because we are daydreaming of a future in fantasy. I will probably live to finish this paragraph. If my prediction turns out to be true, then that does not make my ideas about the future more than mental. A moment in the future to come will be distinct from any thought about it. I avoid missing the moment by not belittling *this instant* by comparing it to a fantastic criterion. Let's distinguish this advice from concentrating our attention upon a single point to the exclusion of anything else. To compare any moment with what never happened and then find it lacking is hubris. Well, it seems that my prediction turned out to be true... *this time.*

> **Culprit, you've missed**
> **your human birth.**
> **Many owners share this body.**
> **Parents say, "Our son!"**
> **and raise him for their profit.**
> **Woman says, "My dear!"**
> **and devours him like a tigress.**
> **Fond wise and loving sons sit,**
> **their mouths gaping like death.**

> Crows and vultures think
> about death, dogs and hogs
> eye the road.
> Fire says, *I'll burn the body.*
> Water says, *I'll quench the flames.*
> Earth says, *I'll mingle with it.*
> Air says, *I'll blow it away.*
> You think that's your home, fool?
> It's the enemy at your throat.
> Dazed by swarms of sense-forms,
> you call the flesh your own.
> The body has so many sharers,
> born and dying in pain.
> Insane, entranced, unthinking man
> shouts "Mine!" and "Mine!" again.

TBoK PP88

Our assumptions about the self create different meanings for the word 'mine.' Anything false must be conceptual because untruth exists only in thought. We act as if our stories of self are our identities and any such narrative includes beliefs about what the satisfaction of our wants means about us. More subtly, we give *unrealized* desires a meaning that reflects our sense of self. The knowledge of how these dubious assumptions induce suffering has great value when that understanding stops the anguish.

> The one who sits is a grocer.
> The one who stands is a milkman.
> The one who stays awake is a nightwatch.
> Death grabs and devours them all.

TWS PP186

Why does Kabir continually goad us with the unavoidable? What is the point? He does not want us to miss what we can and do have. Unfortunately, our desire for consolation robs us of the jewels.

**My eyes brim with tears
as I watch the mill grind:
when the twin stones turn in the mortar,
no one passes through intact.**

TWS PP182

Things we rarely consider, such as a cook who prepares our meals, possess more power over what happens the following day than our plans. The same holds true for other drivers on the road and the pilots of our planes. Now, consider natural events, from the unconscious activity of the cells in our body to the blowing wind, rushing waters, burning forests or quaking earth. We can easily understand the impertinence of our cunning tactics and rituals in one single instant.

**Dear Swan, where will you go when you've left the lake?
You who picked up pearls with your beak in the middle of the lake,
I've helped you find so many moments, so many shades of pleasure
and play.
Now the lake is dry, the lotus leaves have given up their water
drops, the lotuses have lost their freshness.
Kabir says, after parting this time, when will we meet again?**

TWS PP168

The swan stands for each conscious incarnation of *matter* itself. An invitation extends to us to embrace the fullness of life in the mention of death. We are not consoled to believe that any experiences have secret meanings. Our pains and joys pass without denoting anything about who we are.

This lyric of tender affection for life itself gives a sweet gift. A little maturity recognizes that these poems are not the poems of a eunuch, but a man who knows many shades of pleasure and play and also that these delights will end. While offering a glimpse of a beautiful and courageous life that he watched recede long ago, he leaves us with a query that takes courage to answer as we have no reason to believe we will live beyond this life.

It's hard to be born a human:
you won't be born another time.
The ripe fruit that falls to the ground
doesn't grow back on the branch.

TWS PP182

Why imagine a paradise through ornamented gates of pearl or gardens watered by running streams lavished with delicious fruits and dark-eyed virgins? Why dream of countless lives where we can continue to experience through the ages? If we are devoted to a life beyond death, then we sacrifice the existence we actually have to an idea. Vitality pours into wishful thinking, while we gamble for a fantastic future. This weakness becomes worse when we torture ourselves by stomping on harmless joys to acquire a life beyond our reach. As long as we allow authority to direct our imagination into fantastic fictions and use the induced emotion as proof of the ideas, we will be suckers for the power of unfounded beliefs. Swept away in the current of thought our sovereignty goes unnoticed like the sky hidden behind tumultuous clouds.

That which you see is not: and for
that which is, you have no words.
Unless you see, you believe not: what
is told you you cannot accept.
He who is discerning knows by the word;
and the ignorant stands gaping.
Some contemplate the Formless, and
others meditate on form: but the
wise man knows that Brahma is
beyond both.
That beauty of his is not seen of the
Eye : that meter of his is not heard
of the ear.
Kabir says: "He who has found both

**love and renunciation never
descends to death."**

SoK PP95

When we define transience through superstition, we fall below our capacity. Our minds, like a machine that counts coins, places people, things and experiences into known categories. We sift with our preconceived notions and exclude many things that do not fit into our classes, just as the counter mechanically rejects foreign currency. We may understand better by contemplating some horribly misguided choices of our uninformed ancestors 200 years ago. At that time, the murderous Catholic Inquisition still functioned in Spain. Now consider the differences between them and us today. How almost impossible it is to even imagine that 200 years from now, assuming that human life remains on this planet, we might seem as ignorant to our progeny as do our brute forbearers seem to us. We who take thousands of innocents dead as collateral damage in war to be normal and prison rapes seem implicit in punishment. Regardless, the experience of life today can force us beyond our categories when we permit ourselves to see our arbitrary limits.

Let's clarify the word 'Brahma' to mean the consciousness that we must assume in any experience. Something abides in the midst of any observation that remains when the experiences pass. We cannot catch hold of it, but to deny it would be a lie.

We create internal conflict by arbitrarily limiting the aspects of our nature. If we identify with form, then we forsake the formlessness and vice versa. However, why choose one or the other? We observe thought and sensations come and go within a self that no one denies, but also cannot define. Thus, identification with mental activity must be misplaced. After all, if we still exist in the absence of these things, even briefly, then these features cannot truthfully be who we are.

You simple-minded people!

As water enters water,

so Kabir will meet with dust.
"That Maithili pandit said
you'd die near Magahar.
What a terrible place to be dead!
If you want Ram to take you away,
die somewhere else instead.
Besides, they say
whoever dies at Magahar
comes back a donkey."
So much for your faith in Ram.
What's Kashi? Magahar? Barren ground,
when Ram rules your heart.
If you give up the ghost in Kashi
is there some debt
on the Lord's part?

TBoK PP75

Kabir mentions Kashi, a holy place with its promise of liberation if one dies within the city. It seems long ago the municipality conspired with the religious and successfully employed a marketing strategy to peddle salvation. Our poet doubts talk about mortality. He knows the fantasies that enthrall the gullible will not seduce one who does not label the self. Circumstances have loaned us everything we have. We cannot possess anything and do not even control most of what goes on in our own bodies, yet we identify our body with our self. Any renunciation that we might claim must account for experience. It is identity that we can call fictional not the world we are trying to understand through our hypothetical ideas.

I AM neither pious nor ungodly,
I live neither by law nor by sense,
I am neither a speaker nor hearer,
I am neither servant nor master,
I am neither bound nor free,

> I am neither detached nor attached,
> I am far from none: I am near to none.
> I shall go neither to hell nor to heaven.
> I do all works; yet I am apart from
> all works.
> Few comprehend my meaning: he who
> can comprehend it, he sits
> unmoved.
> Kabir seeks neither to establish nor to
> destroy.

SoK PP125

The concept of 'I' is a complex of thought. We need not allow such abstraction to direct us by force of habit. This ego would rather imagine an eternity of hell-bound tortures than admit that there will be an end. Seek not refuge in an idea of reincarnation. One moment of the quiet mind shows these dreams to be what they really are.

> Dying, dying, the world keeps dying,
> but no one knows how to die.
> No one dies in such a way
> that he won't die again.

TBoK PP128

If you can live, knowing that you will probably die once, without eternity to fall back on, perhaps you will not squander your life.

> It's the kind of speech
> no eye can see.
> Kabir says, listen
> to the word spoken
> in everybody.

TBoK PP99

Mortality speaks through us all eventually. Regardless of our differences, we have so much in common. What does this recognition suggest to us about our life today? A thousand times he repeats this life is the jewel and not the moment to come!

Don't be vain, Kabir:
you're just a wrapping of skin on bone.
Even those who ride on horses, under parasols,
are buried quickly in the mud.

TWS PP175

We must imagine the admiration of others in order for vanity to have any meaning. We hide our egoism with its desire to say "look at me," along with our fear of disapproval, which is frequently just the other side of wanting praise. Kabir admits that this desire is whispered in his mind. He watched the crowd dazzled as it gazed upon the yogis contorting themselves, the rich in their finery, the religious with their extravagant rituals and the scholars with their mind numbing oratory. When the river swells beyond the banks, everyone alike, rich and poor, the sacred and profane, must flee and those who fail to escape drown in the mud.

The people of the past were not so unlike us, although their fashions were different. Who has not stumbled or farted something more than wind? Who does not look silly in the morning and have stinking breath? We have all probably believed something untrue and even propagated it to the misfortune of others. In our imaginations, we have probably exalted people with sensational qualities that they do not actually possess. Our tabloid market exposes our obsession with glory. We attribute our own desires to those people who captivate our attention. The idolatry, in turn, inspires imitation. "If 'I' could only be more admired, then 'I' would..." and we fill the blank with a proxy self.

Men display their strength or power and women display their looks. The religious parade their beliefs and children yell, "look at me!" The difference between the young and old seems only to be the sophistication of such efforts. Without an audience, these labors are worthless. Commercial and spiritual marketing exploit this vulnerability by promising exaltation in the future or the next life.

If you're a fish you can't escape:
the fisherman is your death.
Whatever puddle you paddle in,
there you'll meet the net.

TBoK PP116

Life will take from us our abilities and, eventually, our family and friends. We should not be casual with this fact. Even the ability to think will be lost. It only takes time. This terminal diagnosis is also our emancipation. Kabir shows us that nothing really reinforces our sense of self. His other verses invite us to inquire into our awareness without reference to any of those things that appeal to vanity. Do not use meditation as a way to generate desired experiences or as a display of piety for others. A quiet mind removes obstacles and reveals the traps set for us by our own thoughts. Moments of silence liberate us from our habits. The absence of mental habits allows us to see choices that we would not otherwise have considered.

Wooden structure, black termite,
eating all he can.
Death dwells in the body.
No one understands.

TBoK PP101

The destroyer of pretense is death and levels even the greatest kings. Grasp the meaning of this poor weaver who lived in a world just as deadly as our own. When people who have more than they (will ever) need still spend their lives struggling for more, we can see that nothing they have previously acquired has truly satisfied them. What we think we are, who we think we should be and how we want others to see us turns us into slaves of our own imagination. And we pretend that we cannot do anything else but pursue our dreams. We seek a life mentally envisioned at the expense of the life we have, like marionettes tethered to fantasy. Our death is a great ally, but life also offers choices beyond our habits of the mind.

When we seek to find who we are in the things we can accumulate, we move those belongings with us like a dung beetle rolling a ball of shit. This shit becomes an inheritance for our children to fight over as they decide to burn or bury us. They should make this choice of cadaver disposal before we begin to stink.

> **You have died and you will die,**
> **headless and skull-hollow.**
> **Stretched out groaning under a tree,**
> **you'll die today or tomorrow.**

TBoK PP112

How many times has our ego died? No thing or experience can ever really reinforce identity. Who are we without reference to any of our ideas? Meditation gets confused with a way to generate preferred states or tricks to display to impress others. It can also remove the impediment to many available choices. Keeping quiet can liberate us from our habits, one of which is the ideal that "If 'I' could only be or have (some desire), then 'I' could be my true 'self'."

> **The three worlds are a cage,**
> **virtue and vice a net.**
> **Every creature is the pray,**
> **and one hunter:**
> **Death.**

TBoK PP91

No accomplishment thwarts the destroyer of delights. Both the self-torturing ascetic seeking liberation and the sense seeking hedonist want freedom. Daydreamers also receive mortality as a compensation for life. Death remains the great exposé, snatching away any pretense that we hold in our minds, but life also reveals what is changeable. Why accept restraints that will limit our discovery when we weave them ourselves of nothing more than thought?

Brother, why do you strut about,
so full of yourself?
How come you've forgotten
those ten months
when you were suspended
upside down
inside the womb?
When the body's cremated,
it turns to ashes;
when it is buried,
it's eaten by an army of worms.
The body's a jar of unbaked clay
containing water-
that's its greatest claim to fame.
As a honey bee
accumulates its honey,
so a man accumulates his wealth.
But when he's dead, the others say,
Take him away, take him away!
Why have we let this corpse
lie here so long?
His wife accompanies his bier
from the inner rooms to the threshold;
beyond that, his friends bear him away.
The folks in his family
go as far as the cremation ground.
Beyond that,
the swan's all alone.
Kabir says, listen, O creatures,
those fall into
the well of death
ensnare themselves

in make believe Maya,
like parrots who delude themselves
and fall into a bird-catcher's trap.

TWS PP112

If we pass our time waiting for our real lives to begin, then we are missing our real lives, this wasted opportunity is Maya's trap. When a friend dies, we remember that death has embarked on a journey to knock on our door, too. Our image of ourselves in the future often presumes either ongoing redundancy or some excellence that surpasses our present. The many versions of our imagined future motivate our actions today. We fantasize about the lives of powerful people or celebrities forgetting how life can really be. When one of the largest recorded tsunamis in history hit the shores of Asia on December 26, 2004, death made no distinction between the rich and poor and did not discriminate based on religious beliefs.

We know the lovers in a sexual fantasy are not real, as they engage our imagined selves, but thoughts may have a powerful influence on our bodies. Remember that either redundancy or strong sensation will generate habits and such fantasies can do both. The poor architect must constrain his plans to the laws of physics, but our daydreams have no such limit. When our fantastic visions motivate our actions, we guide ourselves by what never really happened. This infirmity goes even further when someone, perhaps a therapist, suggests what life might be like if the past were different or if our childhood were *normal.* Seduced by what never happened, we blame others for robbing us of the joys we did not receive. Remember that there is no end to what never happened. Some people may spend years in therapy processing the emotions resulting from the non-factual.

Why is the doe thin
by the green
pool? One dear,
a hundred thousand

hunters. How to escape
the spear?

TBoK PP91

When circumstances seem to coincide with our prejudices, we feel knowledgeable. However, we should doubt what we imagine about ourselves, otherwise we are fools inviting slaps. Contemplate this true story.

Ron makes a fair living operating a septic company. Once, he serviced the home of a rich executive in a gated community. The client explained with pride that he dug up his own tank for some exercise. The two chatted amicably as the pumping began. Ron noticed some things in the tank, but he never mentioned what he saw. The owner pointed and asked, "Is that what I think it is?" Ron said yes. Someone flushed several condoms from inside his home. From the palpable angst, it seemed that he and his wife did not use condoms. Nothing more was said. A few weeks later, Ron received a call to pump the tank again. A new batch of condoms emerged and the displeased client stopped the work. He handed Ron a wad of cash and indicated he wanted the personal details kept secret. Then, this fellow jumped into his car and left a long trail of smoking rubber. I cannot imagine his wealthy neighbors approved of such reckless driving. Ron's client might have missed the relevant contents of the tank and, to this day, feel quite satisfied in his marriage. This story shows the poverty that wealth cannot halt. How many of our own ideas rest on similar grounds? It would be foolish to think that some of our precious beliefs are not as vulnerable to facts as the poor executive above.

I will add an irony to this story for me personally. From my point-of-view, I only fault the executives' wife for her deception. However, protecting her husband and herself from disease by using condoms deserves merit and, on this score, I count her as a wonderful woman. Could the security this man felt about his marriage before he saw the condoms be as unreal as it was after? I think so. The delusion of a successful person can still shatter under the pressure of a fact. The executive appears to have sought security in circumstances that would doubtlessly be enviable to many. A moment of conviviality shattered his security when he noticed a fact. We cannot avoid such errors of thought through wealth, education or anything we can attain.

Clarity need not elude a capable person. We need not use any circumstance as evidence of identity. When we define ourselves, we more or less play a role construed according to our description of ourselves and respond to the appropriate cues. We submit to associations born of the past that we hold in a questionable memory. We spend our lives trying to create circumstances that seem to sustain the ego. Perhaps this effort to prop up a fictional self is why we cannot print enough money to satisfy an ambitious person. The insatiable desire might be for anything.

One way or another, circumstances change and, if we see ourselves reflected in them, we feel shocked by change. We miss a great deal in such a life because so much that seems worthwhile or even possible must fit inside our tiny teacup of ideas and life need not obey such arbitrary limits.

Everyone went from here
with loads and loads piled on.
Nobody came from there.
Run and try to ask.

TBoK PP121

People will disperse our possessions near the time of our death, if not before. Yet, we try to use these things as evidence of who we are. This recognition is not against using things, but, instead, exposes the ridiculous inference we often try to draw from those things. We receive praise from others for such a futile pretense as identifying with our car or spouse or children. Nothing forces us to believe in such nonsense.

Good Company

Good company engenders happiness,
bad company breeds sorrow.
Kabir says, head for the place where you're sure
to find the true community.

TWS PP184

Who can we trust? Someone with a delightfully agreeable temperament can be deluded and a group can be composed of any number of these people. Also, a wolf dressed as a lamb eats more than grass. Anyone who can imitate or promote popular beliefs receives respect from the crowd. Personal integrity is about separating the chaff from the wheat or purging the errors from our beliefs. The people who can help us with that task are our critics. Don't confuse the truthful exposing of error with the kind of competition that is only interested in winning an argument regardless of truth or falsehood.

Good company not only loves to enjoy life, but also values a difficult truth over a falsehood that may be more appealing. Here are a few hints: such people are both skeptical and willing to try new things. They will not give unearned credit or withhold it when it is due. They will not be afraid to make mistakes. They will risk losing a friend in order to help the same one.

How many days have passed
craving what's savorless?
Seeds don't sprout in barren ground
though torrents pour from the clouds.

TBoK PP110

The desire for a truer grasp of reality can be the only valid definition of spirituality. Any alternative would be moving toward delusion. Our world includes what exists in it, but, from that truism, we should derive that our adaptation to what is true is more useful than becoming accustomed to falsehood. If we want more accurateness, then nothing should be a taboo subject of discussion, especially beliefs that direct our actions. Good company will not shy away from difficult subjects or hide in propriety. To reject the pointed parts of reality leads to minimizing or pretending that they do not exist. Regardless, those thorns will still penetrate our vulnerable skin.

> **Explain, but he won't understand;**
> **he's sold to another's hand.**
> **I'm pulling him toward me,**
> **he's rushing to Deaths City.**

TBoK PP117

The fear of individuals in bondage to ideas is great and even greater when the beliefs that subject them are the only thing they know. A person so enthralled cannot imagine much beyond the choices that have become second nature. It is also an unseen habit to fear any alternative to what we have become accustomed, what we call normal. Our habits combined with a fear of the unknown literally consist of less matter than a silken thread. Still something of less substance than a strand of silk can bind us, if we believe it. The strength of our own imagination is the real binding force when the chains consist of nothing else.

> **A person of quality seizes quality.**
> **One of no quality hates quality.**
> **Give nutmeg to a bullock.**
> **Will he understand? Will he eat?**

TBoK PP120

The unvarnished honesty of excellence is not vulgar or a threat. Liars have difficulty listening to the truth; they say such veracity is foolish and cannot exist in this world. Deceivers will be, or pretend to be, unconvinced regardless of any facts. For a hypocrite, it is easier to dismiss, deny, denigrate or destroy another instead of facing one who loves speaking truthfully.

> **Listen to everyone,**

> **keep your own counsel.**
> **The powder-box holds powder**
> **and has its own cover.**

TBoK PP118

You are the responsible one in your own life. People, who don't want responsibility for their actions, be they rich or poor, will seek authority. Cowards seek authority in both individuals and groups. When the results of giving away personal sovereignty are profitable, these cowards take personal credit for deferring to authority. On the other hand, the authority granted influence receives the blame when the results are unsatisfactory. This system is extremely convenient and encourages vulgar cowardice. Undeserved deference and admiration is part of what Kabir means by being lost in others.

> **I don't touch ink or paper,**
> **this hand never grasped a pen.**
> **The greatness of four ages**
> **Kabir tells with his mouth alone.**

TBoK PP111

Remember Kabir's admonishment about words. They are not the reality, not even his words. We can never cook anything on the word 'fire.'

> **Don't display your diamond**
> **in the vegetable stalls.**
> **Tie it in the knot of the natural,**
> **go your own way.**

TBoK PP109

The word 'natural' is misleading. Even a delusion occurs within nature. Wrap your diamond in the clearest truth you know how to speak. If you find a better cloth to protect the jewel, then abandon the old for the new.

In spite of wanting the best for others, Kabir cannot offer the truth to everyone. A fanatic will kill. A person with power can destroy a poet.

The man with a stake in religion will say that Kabir is going to hell and everyone who listens is at risk. The charlatan will speak more than just lies, he will use just enough of the truth to make his lies seem realistic.

> **The lonely women wave wicks-**
> **Let me see you, Ram!**
> **If you show up after I die,**
> **what's the use?**

TBoK 121

Those individuals who say that they do not have an occasion for self-inquiry probably have time for misery and probably more for amusements. Our choices are not only about what is available, but whether or not we avail ourselves of what is available. If we are not receptive, then the benefits we miss might as well not exist. Sometimes lonely people feel longing for each other but they will not let it show for fear of consequences. Shy lovers are not merely afraid of rejection, they are also afraid of what happens if the other says yes!

> **If I speak out I'm beaten.**
> **When the veil's up, no one sees.**
> **The dog hides under the haystack.**
> **Why talk and make enemies?**

TBoK PP111

Regardless, Kabir did talk, he was beaten and he did make enemies. His beauty, insights and warnings to others came at a cost. Against the tide of superstition, what can one man do? We can understand his doubts about taking the chance.

> **Why waste your words on a fool?**
> **Why teach control to a brute?**
> **Why shoot your arrows at a rock?**
> **You'll only ruin the point.**

TBoK PP110

We only have a small amount of time. Kabir recommends that we do not waste it. A difference exists between real skepticism and saying no. For a man like Kabir, talking to others is like a triage. There are folks who have an immediate pressing need. There are people who can wait and, then, there are those individuals who are, frankly, a waste of time. It is the latter who are lamented in this verse.

> **What can the poor guru do**
> **if the students a lout?**
> **Teach until you're blue,**
> **you're blowing through bamboo.**

TBoK PP127

There is no need to force feed one who feels hungry. If we cook our best for someone and they throw it away, then it may not be our cooking. Offer the food to someone who will eat and be happy for it.

> **They don't listen to wise words**
> **and won't think for themselves.**
> **Kabir continues to scream.**
> **The world goes by like a dream.**

TBoK PP96

The advantage of habits is that we do not need to think to act. Habits can be cheap to demonstrate, but cost a great deal more in the end. Remember our habits, beliefs, expectations, generalizations, prejudice and routines have one thing in common: a prediction.

> **No customers for the word:**
> **the price is high.**
> **Without paying you can't get it,**
> **so move on by.**

TBoK PP 32

The price he asks is a discontinuity with beliefs about ourselves. This sacrifice of the ego is not abandoning facts. It instead doubts the reasoning based on the delusional ideas about who we are.

> **Homage to the one**
> **who knows and tests.**
> **The master gave sugar,**

the fool saw salt.

TBoK PP105

Those individuals who refuse to listen to what they don't already know obviously presume to know the truth already. If that is so, then they should share and welcome scrutiny. Such people often fill the coffers of the flatterers in robes and their pride shines like a jewel. When a friend points out a flaw, they think it an insult, so they seek out the like-minded who know how to show *respect*.

I cry for the world
no one cries for me.
Only he cries for me
who can discern the world.

TBoK PP110

Understand the pain of watching our brothers and sisters torture themselves for nothing. This vision of useless misery is one reason this weaver became a poet. So many beliefs are like mosquitoes that suck our blood while we are unaware. Kabir tried to make people aware of problems that many would not acknowledge. It is pain to see others in anguish especially when they are creating the misery themselves.

Kabir goes on shouting,
perched on a sandal tree.
I show the road, they don't take it:
what's the loss to me.

TBoK PP95

Here is a willingness to love beyond the bounds of propriety. Kabir may be blunt with his affection, but it is an invitation. He will not force anyone to do anything. He invites; he does not use violence. If we request another join us in a celebration, then we cannot insist they accept. Love is not a tyrant. People can choose to give a lover a reason to shed tears and the one who loves would not have it any other way.

The madman without a guru
blindly rushes around,

> **douses the fire on the garbage heap**
> **and burns his own house down.**

TBoK PP118

If we wish to be sensible, then we will subject our preconceived ideas to the same scrutiny that we impose on any criticism of those beliefs; however, this situation is not what typically happens. We see bigots defending their ignorance. Tyrants excuse their use of power. Con men will not trust others. Young people imagine all will be well if they find a spouse and settle down. People learn to imitate those individuals they admire. They should have asked themselves first if those ideas were worthy of reproduction. But to answer the previous question, we must watch someone closely who we admire, then we can see the results. This investigation of others is quite different than imagining the results.

> **Thinking you were of the swan's race,**
> **I sought your company.**
> **If I'd known you were a crazy crane,**
> **I wouldn't have let you touch me.**

TBoK PP120

The words of sages become grease in the hands of fools masturbating their egos. Are you paying money to watch or are you joining in the circle jerk? Our choices cannot be lived vicariously.

> **The world's a pit of soot:**
> **the blind fall right into it.**
> **I sacrifice myself for those**
> **who're stuck in there, yet succeed in climbing out.**

TWS PP175

The blind he refers to are those people who fell into the influence of the unworthy without having a chance to hear something else. We can't speak to such people and not get dirty. Kabir descended into the pit and struggled to help others who could not help themselves. Those individuals who fell into the pit were destined to be food for parasites. Ponder what Kabir's enemies might say against him and you will understand what he means by soot.

You don't find:
diamonds in storerooms,
sandal trees in rows,
lions in flocks,
holy men in herds.

TBoK PP109

People with integrity seek each other out, but not everyone is up for the fiery love of truth. However, anyone can say he seeks truth. Such people associate with each other and blow smoke up each other's asses. It is good for their business, especially when that business caters to the gullible.

Who knows me,
I know him.
I don't care what the world
or the Vedas say.

TBoK PP113

It is difficult to forget the one who tells you the truth. We see in such a man or woman our own reality and it can be both beautiful and terrifying. Someone who knows what delusion is, and the way out, will also have human limitations that others fear to admit.

If you're a true merchant,
keep a true store.
Sweep the inner floor
and throw the garbage far.

TBoK PP97

The more intense the emotion, the more we feel justified in imposing our feelings, even if we generate those feelings through fiction. Christians burned people before the public eye believing they were witches and heretics. In relationships, countless men and women have endured derision and violence from a lover for imagined reasons.

Our prejudices will operate automatically unless we have a pressing reason to arrest them. We will dare attempting trial and error when we must. Ridding ourselves of errors, including the mistakes of past generations, is to remove the rubbish; the alternative is to live in a mental garbage dump.

> **Your wisdom, when you teach a fool,**
> **drops from sight.**
> **Use a ton of soap, but coal**
> **won't turn white.**
>
> TBoK PP108

Kabir's poem above is a lament born of a failure. When others discard his most precious gift, Kabir scolds himself as a reminder not to repeat the mistake. He has many poems to the same effect. It seems that love compelled him to try repeatedly. Those individuals who have the vision to see beyond the limits of the morality in their own era can take heart from his self-admonishment. Look for fertile soil into which to plant the seeds of better ethics.

Prejudice inhibits many from hearing intelligence spoken by a poor, illegitimate craftsman of the lowest caste. I can understand why Kabir would try, even when it seemed hopeless. He also bathed in pools of ablution, worshipped statues and read the holy writ. The people who misunderstood him are not different than he once was. He could never know for sure whether people might understand what they did not the day before. That is why he continued to try. I will not fault him for the attempt because, sometimes, something changes.

> **Man in his stupid**
> **acts-iron mail from head to toe.**
> **Why bother to raise your bow?**
> **No arrow can pierce that.**
>
> TBoK PP108

A human being can rationalize just about anything when he has given himself over to the imagination, be it his own or that of another.

This tendency to justify delusion is as true now as it was in Kabir's day. The rituals, offerings and sacrifices for the sake of an imagined benefit that were present in Kabir's era were founded on the same type of wishful thinking that supports many beliefs of our day.

Son of a slut!
There, I've insulted you.
Think about getting on the good road.
You don't even dream of meeting
the master of your house.
Brahmin, Kshatriya, Bania
don't listen to what I say.
Yogi's and creeping creatures
follow their own way;
and Yogi's at their leisure
don't withdraw
from pleasure.

TBoK PP75

You may notice that strong language calls for attention. Does anyone benefit from such a rebuke? I remember working alongside my father, who could be quite abrupt when calling my attention to danger. Those admonitions left an impression that is still with me. It would be false to the truth to say that I enjoyed those warnings or that I did not wish, at the time, that they had been gentler. Yet, I cannot say that they were not to my benefit.

Clear things one at a time,
whatever can be cleared.
Whoever speaks with two mouths
gets slapped hard.

TBoK PP97

Kabir is patient, despite knowing that time is short. He knows life itself, with its sudden changes, is a brutal teacher! Life can teach what we will not hear. His invitation to meet life on realistic terms seems rude to people when they believe in lies. We childishly play hide-and-seek with death and pretend that tomorrow will come and then we will become honest and will love. We create a hell today by living for tomorrow.

For a person of integrity, each time life shatters a belief, the desire to avoid falsehoods grows stronger. When someone sustains a concept of themselves at the expense of facts, they will stand on their beliefs. Yet, a concept does not abide anywhere, but in the mind. The ego is like a mist. In the bright sunlight of awareness, it disappears.

Those individuals who offer ego fulfillment through spirituality frequently suggest a long process of learning before the benefits can happen. The secret is that people spend lots of their money and often die before receiving their so-called benefits. To those individuals who profit from human misery and suggestibility, I say that death will snatch away anything that they have gained by such sleight-of-hand. To the seekers, I say that before they spend any money, remember that time is the treasure that they cannot replace. I once heard Papaji[xv] tell a group of seekers, "truth can be given with a kiss or a slap, but a slap is better." One reason this statement has merit is that a kiss is lovely. Yet, a kiss can be misunderstood. It is difficult to misunderstand a slap.

Wise, subtle, skillful people!
A single cleverness isn't clever.
A double cleverness misses the point
(creation, destruction, day, night).
They've turned it into a retail business-
rules, piety, self-control, God.
A lord like Hari can't be forsaken,
yet children sing songs of weddings in heaven.
Where have the dead men gone
who drank the guru's tonics?
Know Ram's name to be your own,
throwaway unreal things.

TBoK PP86

To pretend that there is a heaven and sing about it is to turn away from the truth that we can know. What does not change regardless of illusions? If you wish to be close to reality, then stop drinking the tonics of delusion that may come from a guru or your own imagination. Truth is what remains when we stop playing make-believe. We may not understand it, but we can make the approach by exposing the error of our ideas. Above we finally see that Ram's name is our own. Ram is not some God, Ram is you after you stop pretending to be what you are not.

The embodiment of life remains in us, regardless of what we think about ourselves, as long as we breathe. When our pretensions lead to ruin, when we do not understand or when we find ourselves with much less than we once believed, reality is left intact. The awareness of a mistake does not stop us from learning. We stop identifying with our prior concepts and we can let them wither when life exposes them to be worthless, including our conception of self. Let's not blame ourselves for believing plausible falsehoods, if the contrary facts were unknown to us. On the other hand, let's hold all people responsible for ignoring facts contrary to beliefs.

Listen,

you saints-

I see that the world

is crazy.

When I tell the truth,

people run

to beat me up-

when I tell lies,

they believe me.

I've seen

the pious ones

the ritual-mongers-

they bathe at dawn.

They kill the true Self
and worship rocks-
they know nothing.
I've seen
many masters and teachers-
they read their book,
their Qur'an.
They teach many students
there business tricks-
that's all they know.
They sit at home
in pretentious poses-
their minds are full
of vanity.
They begin to worship
brass and stone-
they're so proud
of their pilgrimages,
they forget the real thing.
They wear caps and beads,
they paint their brows
with the cosmetics
of holiness.
They forget the true words
in the songs of witness
the moment they've sung them-
they haven't heard
the news of the Self.
The Hindu says
Rama's dear to him,
the Muslim says
it's Rahim.

They go to war
and kill each other-
no one knows
the secret of things.
They do their rounds
from door to door,
selling their magical formulas-
they're vain
about their reputations.
All the students
will drown with their teachers-
at the last moment
they'll repent.
Kabir says,
listen,
you saintly men,
forget all this vanity.
I've said it so many times
but nobody listens-
you must merge into
the simple state
simply.

TWS PP161

It is clear that Kabir intends to disgrace the saints. He is skeptical that people will ever listen or change. If they did, the holy ones would need to find real jobs. Why is Kabir getting himself into this trouble, being beaten and taking risks to tell the truth? He speaks for the person who is suffering from a deception, the victim may even know they are deceived, but does not understand how it is happening! Kabir found his way out of the maze called religion, but people rarely listen. People, including rebels, lack integrity and courage as they have also sought identity in opposition to established authority. Rebels often take for granted specious arguments from some *rebel authority*. For some people, it may take more courage to question unfounded beliefs than it takes to kill. Even children learn to be soldiers, but few people teach the young how to question beliefs, particularly beliefs about themselves.

This poem attempts to separate the people who have integrity from the herd. Speaking truthfully becomes the invitation. Cowards will reject the implication the moment Kabir calls their beliefs into question. We have learned to fear and reject facts and reason contrary to what those individuals with power have taught us. Moreover, to admit the deception is to disclose our foolishness. If I realize I am eating something rotten, am I more foolish to admit the mistake or keep eating?

The admission of error is a wound to vanity, particularly when, previously, we thought that our beliefs were special, that our beliefs made us one of God's favorites. Often, today in Western countries, the practice of religious seduction is milder than in the past. This softening of religious dogma seems to be due to the discovery of undeniable facts. The religious doctrines that changed to include more facts deserve credit, but the evolution of religion also seems to be a matter of staying relevant. If a marketing firm stops a campaign because it fails to attract consumers, it is reasonable, but they don't deserve much merit for being progressive.

Kabir also exposed those people who give the saints prestige. Such authority figures are nothing without the credulous giving them power. Authorities teach us to approach belief like a vending machine. We expect to get something back for what we put in. Real vending machines do not always work properly, but, compared to religious beliefs, they are far more reliable. When a snack machine fails, you are just out a little bit of money and you can curse at it and even throw a fit. However, with beliefs, we venture both life and money. The return promised on our investment is a secure sense of self and we can never secure a bundle of ideas. If we invest earnestly and the return proves disappointing, there is a problem. The saints have at least two strategies in countless forms to avoid responsibility. One is to say to the disappointed spiritual customer, you did not fulfill your side of the deal; the devotion possessed a flaw or you are a sinner. The saints offer another solution in the afterlife: then we will get our rewards. If we cannot see this crooked deal for what it is, then we earn the name fool.

Religious authorities often frighten their followers to avoid hearing other *dangerous* beliefs. It is not that they are solely concerned that people might leave and they will lose their milk cow. Instead, they are afraid that people will see the same tricks used by other religions. Religion is not the only institution in the business of selling people doubtful or false beliefs, but, over the centuries, religious groups have become quite adept at adapting like corporations. They exploit available opportunities in moral grey areas. When corporations or religions cross a moral line resulting in a public outcry, they excuse the institutional responsibility by blaming individuals, regardless of institutional benefits resulting from the harm done.

Kabir says, if we want to recognize that which is effortless, then we will have to cease the effort and see what remains. Just for awhile, let's stop insisting our ideas are real. We can use our minds and live without clinging to saints and magical beliefs. New options remain hidden when we pretend to be what we are not. Kabir wanted people to discern the choices beyond the doubtful stories. Kabir's recommendations throughout his poetry will *not* secure a sense of self, but they will create more responsibility. If we try imagining what our lives will be like with our choices governed by our capacity instead of bias, then the conclusion will still be constrained. Where imagination fails, discovery will succeed and we do not get to know beforehand what the outcome will be. Now, that is what I call an adventure.

Nectar in a packet
folded again and again.

If you meet someone like yourself,
dissolve it,
give him a drink.

TBoK 103

Our poet shares how he ended his own useless misery. He offers others a drink of a quiet mind and then lets the people who have tasted it decide for themselves if they want to cling to beliefs. Giving the drink to another is not without risk. Kabir cannot know how another will respond. His willingness to try shines light on his many failed attempts to help and, although he faulted himself, he never gave up. Why? Because the fools he wanted to help were people just like him; they suffered and he wanted to show them how he solved the problem.

In front blazing fire,
in back lush green,
gives you fruit when you cut the root-
homage to that tree.

TBoK 129

Long ago, this man, Kabir, spoke the above verse after living a lush, green life. He knew he could not escape the cutting of his root and that the fire would consume his body. He knew that life goes on without him. Nevertheless, if we value what he left for us and if we will quiet our minds and taste the fruits, then we will give him his homage with pleasure.

Epilogue 1 - Self Inquiry

Having finished illuminating the poems of Kabir such as I am able, I wish to reiterate the point of this effort. My dear reader, please allow me to use the words 'you, your and yourself' to also stand for 'we, us and ourselves.'

The accumulation of knowledge *about* the self might seem important to self-inquiry, but such ideas must remain mental activities. The utility of a mental identity should neither be understated nor overstated, but, regardless, it cannot be who you are. This clarity can be a result of introspection, although it is not common.

I am *not* suggesting the refining of the concept of self by conceiving of it correctly. Instead, quieting the mind turns attention to awareness that concepts come and go within, notice consciousness does not cease to exist due to the absence of, or a change in, identity. If you encounter this *neutrality*, this *quiescence* or whatever we may wish to call inchoate consciousness, then the common tendency is to deem it worthless and desolate. In the spacious awareness nothing of any form remains so we have nothing to value in a typical sense. We cannot correctly appreciate consciousness itself if we try to judge consciousness by the standards of the objects that occur within it. The mistaken value judgment about consciousness itself can take various forms, like the following: "I can't do anything with this neutrality, therefore it's worthless." This conclusion happens without noticing the point of reference we are estimating value from is in the mind, it is an object within consciousness. You may also miss the fact that the concept of 'I' you also refer to is similar to any concept that passes in consciousness. When this prejudice happens, I suggest you are in a habit of looking for a 'self-concept' upon which to cling, like a raft in a boundless ocean. You may safely discard the whole judgment, allowing the inchoate consciousness to remain without judging it by an improper standard. *Any* judgment you may have, right or wrong is secondary and assumes consciousness. The fact that none of us has a good standard to judge consciousness by does not make consciousness worthless. A diamond wont cease to be valuable or useful just because a child my prefer the sparkle of tinsel. My metaphor is not about the value of a diamond but rather mistaken standards of judgment.

When the clarity that you are not your thoughts emerges, you temporarily abandon symbolizing the self, including the thought of 'I', even though these ideas are useful in other circumstances. Moreover, if even one idea disappears or you exchange it with another, this change suggests, and perhaps demonstrates, the hypothetical nature of ideas. The focus of this book suggests that anyone can directly inquire into consciousness and see that all identification is hypothetical.

The belittling of introspection by many astute thinkers resulted from real problems, but went too far. The imagination that attaches meaning to subjective experience is quite wild and doubtful. If you were to concentrate your attention on your foot or the top of your head to the exclusion of anything else, you would likely become aware of especially different sensations. To whatever degree you experience these novel sensations, it will be impossible to tell if the sensation you feel is coming from outside you or has an internal source. These feelings can be quite intense and be experienced through the whole body. It may well be that our more habitual cognitive processes filter out many sensations. The sound of a refrigerator humming in the background we tend to ignore unless we grant it attention. Novel sensation including spiritual experiences may not be new phenomena, but are more like the ticking sound of a clock that we don't hear without focusing on it. It is the creation and interpretation of such states that is the shady-business of spiritual teachers. These spiritual interpretations are often wildly fantastic and not provable. What is of interest here is how to keep people from becoming delusional because of these *interpretations*. The states themselves are *not* inherently bad and there are certain facts that must be true (analytically) for the novel phenomena to be experienced.

For example, any experience that comes and goes within you cannot itself be you.

Inquiry into consciousness shows you what you are *not*, as well as suggesting that you must be something other than any idea. Ideas *about* yourself dissolve in this consideration.

It's a mistake when a skeptic dismisses novel (spiritual) experiences as hogwash just because someone interpreted an experience with vague words, such as the Holy Spirit moving in them, Shakti or Kundalini. This mistake is like tasting bad soup and assuming bad ingredients. The fault might be the cooking, not the ingredients.

Maya and mind are one,
Maya permeates mind.
The three worlds whirl in doubt.
To whom can I explain?

TBoK 101

If we grant knowledge to be hypothetical, then it seems remarkable that a man living in the 15th century could intuitively grasp such an explanation. Above, Kabir boldly asserts that the three worlds whirl in doubt. Kabir's uses the figure of speech "three worlds" referring to Hindu scripture meaning sattva, rajas and tamas interpreted loosely as truth, sensation and delusion. Kabir's comment is simple, the *purist truth*, the *sensual* and the *delusional,* any of these you apprehend through your mind and mistaking any mental reflection for the actual becomes the problem that our poet tries to solve or at least admit.

The distinguished method of science, of testing any thesis in an attempt to *falsify it*, is the most fruitful of human attempts to approach the truth. Many spiritualists try to borrow the credibility of science to support their claims and we, rightly, label this action with the uncomplimentary word 'pseudo-science'. If we cannot test a belief, with the possibility of proving it false, calling the belief scientific in any way is a lie, worse for being so common. I will address this problem further in the following section to skeptics.

"When the wave rises, it is the water;
and when it falls, it is the same
water again. Tell me, Sir, where
is the distinction?"

SoK PP57

Regardless of how you explain or understand consciousness, if you create misery based on fiction, you have a problem. You reason from what you create, a meager abstraction. Still, you are not obliged to believe or obey any ideas of yourself because such concepts cannot be who you are any more than a diagnosis is a disease. I am talking about emancipation from a fictional identity.

"Knowledge ahead, knowledge behind,
knowledge to the left and to the right.
The knowledge that knows what knowledge is:
that's the knowledge that's mine."

TWS Rear Cover

Kabir reminds you not to mistake thought for anything other than mind stuff. Delusion limits your capacity to abide in and adapt to the actual circumstances of life. Let a lion represent habits of mind. It is less helpful to discuss the danger of lions to someone being mauled by one. Yet, the information may be vital for one who does not see one of the beasts stalking him.

Experiences, habits and beliefs need not be an identity.

"Notice the difference between limitation and delusion. Limitation can be called not knowing, not being able, and being prone to mistakes. Delusion alters the truth, even just a little, to keep the ego from being exposed as a bogus notion. Keeping the concept of our self intact becomes a source of motivation to create delusion when those ideas [of self] would be destroyed by something true." [xvi]

Todd Vickers

Epilogue 2 - To Skeptics

I hope this book will interest the skeptic as much as the poet or spiritual seeker. Skeptics may better understand what I say because they, presumably, have fewer superstitions that they desire to have confirmed. A skeptic might pre-judge Kabir's poetry due to contempt for religions that have appropriated his verses. *Note that these religions would be the ones that Kabir criticizes unequivocally.* To those individuals tempted out of habit to look sideways at this poet due to some experiences and negative associations with religious language, I advise you to suspend judgment. Kabir used whatever language he thought understandable, including words associated with the spiritual practices of his day. Still, the man who wrote the following is not beholden to any dogma, belief or tradition.

> **There is nothing but water at the**
> **holy bathing places; and I know**
> **that they are useless, for I have**
> **bathed in them.**
> **The images [gods] are all lifeless, they cannot**
> **speak; I know, for I have cried**
> **aloud to them.**
> **The Purana and the Koran are mere**
> **words; lifting up the curtain, I**
> **have seen.**
> **Kabîr gives utterance to the words of**
> **experience; and he knows very**
> **well that all other things are un-**
> **true.**

SoK PP90

Kabir slaps both spiritual practitioners and those individuals who presume to lead them. We cannot be to often reminded of the courage required to say such things, indeed many people have lost their lives for saying less. Also, the caliphate leaders that ruled India in Kabir's time deserve a salute for their moderation, at least in the case of this poet. Kabir is not merely antagonistic to religion, he speaks about any dogmatic beliefs arising from a concept of self. Consider the beliefs of heaven, hell, reincarnation, success, monogamy or what it means about us to have a lover. These ideas have, at their fulcrums, a concept of a self to whom they are relevant. If that idea of self is what makes the beliefs important, then it is worthwhile to know more about it. Many beliefs, religious or not, are an attempt to stabilize and sustain this self. Beliefs founded upon this mental habit of identification are quite disputable.

Many unbelievers use the word 'God,' but define this word as a statement of natural laws, not a deity. This subtly placates religious people and protects the livelihood of scientists and skeptics by avoiding controversy. Such people would think seriously before making a public statement like Kabir's aforementioned prose. As we noticed in his poems, Kabir challenged beliefs and suffered as a result. Fortunately, he survived regardless of his impiety. Kabir said,

> **"The small ruby everyone wants has fallen out**
> **on the road.**
> **Some think it is east of us, others west of us.**
> **Some say, "among primitive earth rocks," others, "in**
> **the deep waters."**
> **Kabir's instinct told him it was inside, and what**
> **it was worth,**
> **and he wrapped it up carefully in his heart cloth."**

TKB PP44

Kabir writes not only as one in the midst of discovery, but also as one who has known the discontent that plagues humanity. He knows the difference between not understanding and misunderstanding. The former is when we know we do not know. The latter is thinking we know when we do not. He sees the anguish and contends with pride and ignorance, illuminating the same points from many different perspectives.

By imposing beliefs on the world as if they were something more, we often impose an error. People rarely display such hubris as to presume that they know everything. However, it is a common arrogance to view everything only in reference to our beliefs. Humans habitually associate almost everything with what is already in their minds. For example, the fact that I am writing on this particular poet has resulted in me being associated with Hindus, Muslims and a particular New Age Sufi. The people in the aforementioned groups would not be flattered. I am not associated with any tradition. This habit of thinking about things according to our preconceived ideas becomes as automatic as eating with a dominant hand and goes unnoticed. Our preconceived ideas become a problem when they are wrong. Not everything orange is an orange. I suggest vigilance; do not acquiesce to the habit of drawing conclusions from old beliefs. Such a result cannot help, but obscure the point. Perhaps the content of this book is something not yet known.

A raft of tied-together snakes
in the world-ocean.
Let go, and you'll drown.
Grasp, and they'll bite your arm.

TBoK PP103

In the last poem, the raft is the mind, yet the snakes bite when the belief is flawed. Poetry tries to bridge the gap where logic, experience and imagination fail. Poetry seems out of favor these days and I am often sympathetic with this view, but not concerning Kabir. Poetry is derided by some thinkers,[xvii] even to the extent that David Hume called poets "liars by profession."[xviii] Hume's judgment possesses some truth and something deceptive. We cannot savor any sweetness in the word 'apple.' Words are inaccurate; they are something other than what they indicate. This often-unnoticed limitation is common in all languages, including logical symbolism. If those individuals with a profound capacity for reason wished to build a gallows from which to hang the poets for the crime of being loose with words, they would need to tie nooses for their own necks to be consistent.

Words are symbols like notes on sheet music. If you are not a musician, such notes are gibberish, even if you like the songs. Musicians interpret notes according to their level of understanding and skill. Beyond the ink on the paper and the players, the music itself describes something to the listeners. The metaphors of sound invoke feelings in the hearers and, often, that experience is inter-subjective. For example, when we feel tears in our eyes during a symphony, many of us have seen tears in the eyes of others. In music, we can share a poignant, non-rational understanding with others. We perceive musical 'inferences' and the understanding is inter-subjective between people. Not everyone will share the experience but that doesn't mean the experience didn't really happen or is a mass delusion. I cannot make the translations of Kabir's poems consistent. However, as in music, dissonance is often part of a complex song. The rhythm may seem strange, but, if you relax a little, you may feel the pulse of Kabir's verse in time with your own body-mind. You may even want to dance. Kabir comes as close as poetry will allow to clarify a point. Logic attempts this same task with the objective world and, still, we see ourselves stretching the language to its limit.

> "...I shall not confine myself to any one, but shall employ on each occasion the word which seams least likely in the particular case to lead to misunderstanding; nor do I pretend to use either these or any other words with a rigorous adherence to one single sense. To do so would often leave us without a word to express what is signified by a known word in some one or other of its senses: unless

authors had an unlimited license to coin new words, together with (what would be more difficult to assume) unlimited power of making readers understand them. Nor would it be wise in a writer, on a subject involving so much abstraction, to deny himself the advantage derived from an improper use of a term, when, by means of it, some familiar association is called up which brings the meaning home to the mind, as it were by a flash." [xix]

John Stuart Mill

Logic seems out of place as a metaphor for a subjective topic and, particularly, poetry. I am not trying to be strict. I employ the word 'logic' because it seems less likely to lead to a misunderstanding. The moment reasoning indicates something beyond public observation, the language becomes creatively descriptive, metaphoric or symbolic. Analogy is not evidence, but, rather, it indicates a different way of reasoning. Both logic, and poetry for that matter, become just an arrogant means of persuasion if its intention is to deceive us. Any statement not tested against observation gives a reason for doubt, but doubt is not falsification. My dear skeptics please consider this entire work a thesis, the same way we should with any knowledge. If anyone sees a flaw in my use of reason, facts or examples, they are welcome to inform me.

Formalities deserve merit, but are not always necessary. Most of us have observed a helpless baby communicate by pointing at something, like a milk bottle, and crying. The young child is vague and illogical, yet we can understand him. I try to make my points clear, including being reasonable and literal and making some statements not far removed from the example of the above infant. The significance is not of formal structure, but rather the benefit of realizing we are not beholden to our beliefs. I use words as tools within the limits of my command of the language. I cannot dig a hole with the word 'shovel' or its concept.

Does your life suggest that what is included in this book is useful?

Do reason and facts both coincide with the answer to that question?

Whenever someone who is not a scientist, *including myself,* interprets science, we have reason to doubt that interpretation. Remember the difference between falsehood and doubt. A cook can make chowder with good clams, but that doesn't mean it will be worth eating.

As far as I know, we cannot yet prove what consciousness is, for it is difficult to trace to a cause. We are free to interpret test results differently. Let us mention the exceptions to the past results that show us our knowledge is incomplete. I leave inquiry on such matters as the physical mechanics of consciousness to those individuals better suited to discuss it. The problem at issue again is human misery and how we reduce it, particularly when the foundation of so much suffering is more or less fictional. If someone can address this problem in a better way, then let them be a light unto us all.

Regarding self inquiry, any questions involving subjectivity lack the tests that can show a thesis to be false.[xx] Our integrity remains the only defense against desires that tantalize us into delusions that can arise from introspection. Self-inquiry cannot (yet) be a testable science, but it can be rigorous. To treat the knowledge of ourselves and our explanations of subjective experiences as hypothetical gives us a chance to test our ideas using *results.* These results can be different from day-to-day and, although incapable of proving our subjective ideas about ourselves to be universally true, they *can* prove ideas about the self to be universally false when the results are different from what we expected or from previous experience. When a man is red-faced and screaming "I am not angry," his interpretation of the events seems false.

The temptation to dismiss or rule out the consciousness that we cannot accurately conceive favors a thesis that any concept of self is unstable. What we call identity arises and falls continuously within the inchoate being or consciousness that I discuss in this work. I am not trying to prove whether consciousness is a social product built from the stones of language. I am not guessing at whether consciousness is an epiphenomenon or a complex biological algorithm. Human misery, particularly when that suffering is born of imagination, is an important problem whether or not consciousness is nothing more than a function of neurons and bio chemistry. Regardless of how we try to explain consciousness, the reduction of manufactured human misery is valuable.

Epilogue 3 - Kabir's Questionable Admirers

After reading various translations and works on Kabir, I grew annoyed with one author in particular who used the statements of *saints* as commentary on Kabir. Cobbling together the words of religious authorities gives an author license to say anything without taking any personal responsibility if some religious figure said it first. Nothing *anyone* has ever said is beyond question. There are few absurdities so out of bounds that some holy person somewhere has not supported them, including the justification of mass murder.

Perhaps some individuals who admire Kabir cannot resist endearing him to people who admire popular spiritual authorities. Such authors seek and find some language that overlaps, more or less, and then equate those statements and the individuals who said them with Kabir, as if the content were similar. This tactic brings no new understanding, but, rather, suppresses the faculties of ordinary mortals by appealing to arbitrary authority. This homogenizing happens even with the words of those individuals who recommended death for the kind of impiety displayed by Kabir. I see such an interpretation to be directly in opposition to the content of his poems.

When granting the aforementioned authors the benefit of the doubt, I suspect that they wanted either to share Kabir with more people or bring the religions of the world together on common ground, perhaps giving the more passionate followers a chance to stop killing each other. It is not such an intention that I fault, but, rather, the consequences. It confers admiration due to Kabir upon those individuals who are undeserving; it places our poet in the company of those individuals that his work intentionally discredits. Perhaps it is just a ridiculous overreach of a well-intentioned author. I do not understand why admirers of Kabir abase his work in this way! If I withdraw my more generous interpretation, I suspect that such writers are like the greedy dairy farmers who mixed melamine with milk,[xxi] giving it the appearance of being more wholesome and, as a result, poisoning their customers.

Other Works by the Author

Vickers, Todd. *The Paradox of Self Realization.* Felton: Vickers Publications, 1999.

Vickers, Todd. *Truth Like Fire.* Felton: Vickers Publications, 2001.

"No Shame in Sex," Todd Vickers, accessed January 3, 2015, http://www.noshameinsex.com.

Recommended Reading

Barnum, P.T. *The Humbugs of the World: an Account of Humbugs, Delusions, Impositions, Quackeries, Deceits and Deceivers Generally, in All Ages.* Seattle: Amazon Digital Services, Inc., 2012.

Bentham, Jeremy. *The Rationale of Reward.* New York: Evergreen Review, Inc., 2008.

Briffault, Robert. *Psyche's Lamp: The Illusion of Individuality.* Ann Arbor: University of Michigan Library, 1921.

Burnet, John. *Early Greek Philosophy.* New York: Meridian Books, 1892.

Dennett, Daniel C. *Breaking the Spell: Religion as a Natural Phenomenon.* New York: Penguin Books, 2007.

Harris, Sam. *Free Will.* New York: Free Press, 2012.

Hume, David. A Treatise of Human Nature, Book 1: Of the Understanding. Seattle, Amazon Digital Services, Inc., 2011.

Isacoff, Stuart. *Temperament: The Idea That Solved Music's Greatest Riddle.* New York: Alfred Knopf, 2001.

James, William. *Pragmatism: Full and Fine Text of 1907 Edition.* Seattle: Amazon Digital Services, Inc., 2013.

Kant, Emanuel. *Critique of Pure Reason, 2nd revised ed., In Commemoration of the Centenary of its First Publication.* Seattle: Amazon Digital Services, Inc., 2011.

Mill, John Stuart. *A System of Logic.* London: Longman, 1959.

Poonja, H. W. L. *Wake Up and Roar.* Louisville: Sound True, 2007.

Popper, Karl. *The Two Fundamental Problems of the Theory of Knowledge.* London: Routledge, 2008.

Russell, Bertrand. *The Problems of Philosophy.* Oxford: Oxford University Press, 1912.

Tagore, Rabindranath. *Songs of Kabir.* Newburyport: Red Wheel/Weiser, 2002.

Vickers, Todd. *Truth Like Fire.* Felton, Vickers Publications, 2001.

Notes

[i] Rabindranath Tagore, *Songs of Kabir* (Newburyport: Red Wheel/Weiser, 2002), ix.

[ii] *The Koran* 3:89-91: "But those that recant after accepting the true faith and grow in unbelief, their repentance shall not be accepted. These are the truly erring ones. As for those that recant and die unbelievers, no ransom shall be accepted from them: be it as much gold as would fill the entire earth. They shall be sternly punished. These are the truly erring ones."

[iii] Bertrand Russell, *The Problems of Philosophy* (London, Home University Library, 1912), 63.

[iv] I recommend both Sam Harris and Daniel Dennett and their books discussing consciousness. See the Recommended Reading section for more information.

[v] William James, *Pragmatism* (London, Longmans, Green and Co., 2013),586-7.

[vi] Repeated from my memory of a conversation with Sri H.W.L Poonja in Lucknow, India in 1994.

[vii] "Interview With Condoleezza Rice; Interview With Richard Gephardt," CNN, accessed January 3, 2015, http://transcripts.cnn.com/TRANSCRIPTS/0309/07/le.00.html.

[viii] Todd Vickers, *Truth Like Fire* (Felton, Vickers Publications, 2001), 95.

[ix] Todd Vickers, *Truth Like Fire* (Felton, Vickers Publications. 2001), 94.

[x] **Stuart Isacoff, *Temperament*: *The Idea That Solved Music's Greatest Riddle* (New York: Alfred Knopf, 2001), 47.**

[xi] Quote attributed to PT Barnum. See Recommended Reading section for more information.

[xii] Robert Briffault, *Psyche's Lamp: The Illusion of Individuality* (Crow's Nest: George Allen & Unwin LTD, 1921), 229-230.

[xiii] Todd Vickers, *Truth Like Fire* (Felton, Vickers Publications, 2001), 19.

[xiv] Emanuel Kant, *Critique of Pure Reason* (London: George Bell & Sons, 2011), xxxvi: "The estimate of our rational cognition a priori at which we arrive is that it has only to do with phenomena, and that things in themselves, while possessing a real existence, lie beyond its sphere."

[xv] For more information, see: Sri H. W. L. Poonja, *Wake Up and Roar* (Louisville: Sound True, 2007).

[xvi] Todd Vickers, Truth Like Fire (Felton, Vickers Publications, 2001), 96.

[xvii] Jeremy Bentham, *The Rationale of Reward* (London: Robert Heward, 1830), 64: "Prejudice apart, the game of push-pin is of equal value with the arts and sciences of music and poetry..." – "Everybody can play at pushpin: poetry and music are relished only by a few. The game of push-pin is always innocent: it were well could the same be always asserted of poetry. Indeed, between poetry and truth there is a natural opposition."

[xviii] David Hume, A Treatise of Human Nature, Book 1: Of the Understanding (Boston, Dutton &. Co., 1920), 121: "Poets themselves, though liars by profession, always endeavor to give an air of truth to their fictions; and where that is totally neglected, their performances, however ingenious, will never be able to afford much pleasure."

[xix] John Stuart Mill, *A System of Logic* (Toronto: The University of Toronto Press, 1973), 64.

[xx] For more information, see: Karl Popper, *The Two Fundamental Problems of the Theory of Knowledge* (London: Routledge, 2008).

[xxi] "China Toxin Scandal Moves to Liquid Milk," The Guardian, accessed January 3, 2015, http://www.guardian.co.uk/world/2008/sep/20/china.food.